RELATIONSHIPS
TO INFINITY

RELATIONSHIPS TO INFINITY

THE ART AND SCIENCE OF KEEPING IN TOUCH

JASON LEVIN

NEW DEGREE PRESS

RELATIONSHIPS TO INFINITY

The Art and Science of Keeping in Touch

ISBN   978-1-63730-693-2   *Paperback*

          978-1-63730-783-0   *Kindle Ebook*

          979-8-88504-023-5   *Ebook*

To Lori. Everyday life is better with you in it.

To my wacky sons. Everyday life is funnier with you in it.

Contents

———

Introduction

———

My mom gave me the news while I was on a family vacation with my grandparents in South Florida. She had just gotten off the phone with my dad. He was going to lose his job of twenty years at a New Jersey-based garment manufacturer. It was August 1989, and America was entering a recession. I was starting my sophomore year in high school. In a state of bewilderment, I wondered, "Why is this happening to him? To our family? Will everything turn out all right?" Ultimately, my dad's persistence and my mom's support helped him land another job. I also learned some important life lessons.

The uncertainty that came with my dad's unemployment compelled me to understand more about business and the economy. I became a frequent reader of publications such as *BusinessWeek, Forbes, Fortune,* and The *Wall Street Journal.* In these articles, I noticed recurring themes on career management and how successful executives often referred to their "mentors," "network," and "relationships." I thought to myself, "How does one develop these relationships?" and "What is a network?"

While in high school, I was a babysitter. I began sharing what I was learning with the parents of kids whom I was babysitting. These parents were doctors, lawyers, accountants, actuaries, and financial and sales executives. Each one had their own point of view, but the consensus was clear. Keeping in touch mattered in both your career and life.

THE KEEP-IN-TOUCH JOURNEY BEGINS

My dad's unemployment kept me from traveling with my high school French club on a trip to France. But the idea of going to France stayed with me, and I made a promise to myself: "Jason, go intern in France before college graduation." As I thought through this seemingly improbable idea, I was curious to discover whether my newfound interest in keeping in touch could help me achieve my goal.

With eight months to plan, I shared my France internship dream with everyone I knew. Inspired by my dad's persistence during his job search and my commitment to keeping in touch, I connected with the former speech writer for the U.S. Ambassador to France. This one conversation allowed me to realize the dream: a summer volunteer opportunity in Paris at the US Ambassador's Residence.

The summer of 1996 in Paris was everything I hoped for and more. Following a brief stay in a Paris youth hostel, my boss cleared me to move into the Ambassador's Residence, where I roomed with the cooks and maids. Based on my performance, I was invited to the French Open. I saw Steffi Graf, one of the greatest female professional tennis players of all time, defeat Arantxa Sanchez Vicario in an amazing three sets. One evening, I ate dinner in the restaurant within the Eiffel Tower while the Bastille Day fireworks were going off behind Trocadero Square. That summer in Paris sparked in me a life-long interest in keeping in touch.

WE SAY IT, BUT DO WE REALLY MEAN IT?

"Keep in touch," is in my opinion, one of the most overused and misunderstood phrases in America. People talk about their interest in developing or maintaining a relationship, and yet still they don't. For me, the gap between what is said and what is done is the ultimate paradox.

In my ten years as a coach, I have been continually surprised to see a running theme in otherwise quite successful executives. Whether they come to me with a desire to get a promotion, make a career change, or develop their own professional services practice, there has been one core theme. These talented executives of diverse backgrounds do not emphasize the importance of their own prior relationships. They are not keeping in touch.

In working with my clients, when I mention keeping in touch, they immediately think of networking. The concept of networking can make some executives cringe, creating moments of hopelessness and despair. Executives know it is important, and yet they do not know where to begin. Images of "salesy extroverts" come to mind where somehow an underlying ask is about to be made. Executives feel they need to engage in a black hole of "networking events" and "endless social media posts" to truly network. A belief also exists that you need to come across as super-human during an initial interaction.

As if you need to tout all the great things you have ever done in your career in a first meeting. Movies, TV shows, and social media only further these myths. If you have ever used LinkedIn, you'll likely receive daily invites from people you don't know who want to "connect." They really think they are "networking" with you.

NETWORKING AS NONSENSE

I have long thought the word "networking" is a nonsense word. A catch-all term that says nothing. Networking is thrown out as a magical elixir to solve all career and business development-related problems. This classic networking advice is neither intentional nor genuine. It incorrectly assumes someone you just met off the street or connected with on LinkedIn will drop everything so you can get your next promotion, job, or client. There is a better way through all this noise.

This networking advice ignores the most important asset in your career: the people you already know. You have friends from high school, college, and graduate school. You have former colleagues, vendors, partners, and clients who know the value of your work, your ethics, and your uniqueness. You have volunteered for local civic, religious, political, and social mission nonprofit organizations. They know you as a human being. They have trusted you for important projects. They might have hired you for your advice and counsel. You might have mentored or promoted these people. These people might have mentored or promoted you. After working for twenty-five-plus years, you have scores of people who have relied on you. They know and trust you.

If you are stumped by the idea of networking, begin with the people you already know. This is the best use of time. Don't look left or right; just look in the mirror and go back in time. The pandemic of 2020–2021 has taught us that the foundational human need for connection is alive and well. So let's stop saying "Keep in touch" when we really mean "happy to keep in touch, if you do the work."

THE VALUE OF KEEPING IN TOUCH

The data supports my keep-in-touch observations. According to LinkedIn, 80 percent of professionals consider networking important to career success. Yet, networking attitudes don't match networking behaviors:

1. **Keeping in Touch Is Hard** – 38 percent globally said they find it hard to stay in touch with their network
2. **Time Is the Issue** – The leading cause? Nearly half (49 percent) globally say they don't keep in touch because they don't have enough time.
3. **Actions Don't Align with Beliefs** – Interestingly, despite the majority (79 percent) globally agreeing that professional networking is valuable for career progression, less than half (48 percent) say they keep in touch with their network when things are going well in their career.

I wrote this book because I wanted to understand why people aren't keeping in touch. Success has never been achieved in isolation; rather, it is a team sport. A mentor provides ideas to help you land the client. A prior colleague gives insight into an organization where you might want to land a job. Your team is a valuable, supportive, diverse, and intelligent network. The notion of "self-made success" or "pulling one-self up by one's bootstraps" is a fallacy. In *Give and Take*, Adam Grant refers to research conducted by Brian Uzzi, a management professor at Northwestern University. He states, "Networks come with three major advantages: private information, diverse skills, and power."

Keeping in touch is the core of maintaining these networks. If you are reading this book, you might be thinking, "I am not good at keeping in touch." I agree it is hard to keep in touch. Life events (*e.g.,* marriage, children, divorce, new jobs, illness, aging parents) create natural distance to existing relationships. In addition to life events, the misperception is that the bigger the network, the better the network. Social networks such as LinkedIn, Facebook, and Instagram fuel this notion that you need to "connect," "grow your reach," and "grow your network" as a path to success.

These activities can actually make us lonelier, both professionally and personally. According to Guy Finch in *Psychology Today*, "Loneliness does not depend on how many friends or relationships you have. Loneliness depends entirely on the *subjective* quality of your relationships—on whether you feel emotionally and/or socially disconnected from those around you. In her TEDx Chelsea Park talk on loneliness, Dr. Robin Joy Myers asserts "that while we are more connected through email, text, phone and video conference, we are actually more lonely than ever." Digital networking platforms directly increase the quantity of our relationship set, but they tend to dilute the quality of our relationships. In a true contradiction, digital networking is both a solution and a problem.

Does this mean I don't believe in or have a presence on social media? No, I actually engage with LinkedIn, Facebook, and Twitter. For those with the right intentions, these are incredible tools to share information, connect, and strengthen your personal and professional relationships. Using technology to support underlying human connections can transform our lives.

KEEPING IN TOUCH IS THE SPECIAL SAUCE OF A SUCCESSFUL CAREER

I also feel qualified to write this book because I have seen my clients' success firsthand through coaching, training, and speaking. I've watched executives land new jobs, earn promotions, and make retirement transitions. I've witnessed lawyers, accountants, executive search professionals, and consultants build intentional business development plans and gain new clients. These successes noticeably increased when they stopped "networking" and focused instead on their authentic social network.

In your career, your smarts and technical ability can only take you so far. Counter to the idealistic hope that people are hired and promoted on their accomplishments, the critical separator is actually your relationships. Having a variety of trusted relationships propels careers. Since relationships are so important to job seeking, promotions, and building a professional services practice, keeping in touch is the glue that keeps relationships alive and well. Keeping in touch is the fuel to your relationship vehicle.

When you say "Keep in touch," it can truly mean "Try" and "Make the effort." Plenty of people in your relationship base would like to hear from you. All you need to do is send an email, direct message, text, or pick up the phone.

This book is for executives and emerging leaders looking to take the next step in their careers and who are stuck. What you will learn in this book can be leveraged to:

- Build your authentic social network
- Grow your career in your current organization
- Assist in your career or retirement transition
- Launch your professional services practice

The wonderful thing about the premise behind *Relationships to Infinity: The Art and Science of Keeping in Touch* is that you can always get back in touch. You can always make the outreach and the effort to reconnect. You can take the initiative and own this process for yourself. You can reconnect with people who have been there for you over the years. You can keep in touch or get back in touch. You will find *Relationships to Infinity* to be conversational in tone. This is by design. I see keeping in touch as two ongoing conversations: 1) An honest conversation with yourself on how you approach keeping in touch, and 2) The actual "conversations" you have with your authentic social network.

This book is broken into three parts and eleven chapters. Part One of *Relationships to Infinity* is about making a case for social networks. I review how networks function and how you can leverage them. In Chapter 1, I begin with a story of an executive in finance who discovers keeping in touch is an important part of her career. Her keep-in-touch story is compelling because it demonstrates it is never too late to start.

Simply put, today is a wonderful day to start keeping in touch. Chapter 2 provides an overview of the academic research on network theory, highlighting an important concept called "dormant ties." Dormant ties are people you lose touch with. Reconnecting with your dormant ties can actually be a wonderful opportunity in your career. In Chapter 3, I review the different elements of trust in relationships. Trust does not depend on your personality type. Introverts and extroverts are equally good at building trust.

Part Two leverages research and examples to further explore how we approach relationships. Chapter 4 covers the "Social Fortress" people create for themselves and how it can hold us back from reaching out. At important times in your career, you need to tap into varied perspectives and tear down this fortress. This chapter helps identify ALL the people within your network. Through stories and examples, I provide options for you to tear down your social fortress. Chapter 5 is about friendships and how to make the time to keep in touch with people you care about. Personal or professional or both, making time to keep in touch is critical.

Part Three is about turning ideas into action. Based on my conversations with therapists, I developed the Bermuda Keep-in-Touch Triangle, which I share in Chapter 6. Barriers to keeping in touch exist both in your mind and in society. I provide ideas on how to break through your "triangle." Chapter 7 is about tactically getting back in touch. No, you don't need to apologize. Rather, the research on nostalgia suggests you share positive memories as you reconnect. Chapter 8 helps take your keep-in-touch strategy to a new level by leveraging associations. Chapter 9 teaches you how you can use

LinkedIn to keep in touch. Chapter 10 provides perspectives of successful executives and how keeping in touch has helped them advance in their careers. The final chapter invites you to get started with some tactical ideas and suggestions.

To help you along the way, each chapter in the book ends with a summary and reflection questions. Please take a moment to think through what these ideas mean for you. Write notes in this book and fold back pages. I won't be offended.

Keeping in touch is about simple, consistent actions. Keeping in touch is about authenticity. Keeping in touch is about caring for the people who have helped you along the way. Keeping in touch is about listening. Keeping in touch is being a partner to your trusted circle of colleagues and friends. Let's chart a new path in YOUR keeping in touch journey. You will be glad you did.

CHAPTER 1

You Can Always Start Keeping in Touch

Before we dig into the academic research and keep-in-touch strategies, I'd like to begin with Usha Chaudhary's story. Her life and career paint a portrait of what authentic relationships can really look like. Too many times, I have seen accomplished executives getting so psyched out about keeping in touch they do not know where to begin. This is why I am beginning with Chaudhary. She has "all the right stuff": smart, credentialed, motivated, accomplished, and kind. However, she didn't always keep in touch. It was not on her radar. Even though Chaudhary did not keep in touch in the past, she could still start now. Frankly, she could be any of you, particularly if you have not made keeping in touch a priority.

LIFE EVENTS DICTATE A CHANGE IN CAREER PLANS

The untimely passing of Chaudhary's father changed her world. The oldest of eight children, he has grown up in humble beginnings on a farm in India. He was the first in the family to leave the village and pursue education. Eventually, he became an officer in India's foreign service. During her father's diplomatic missions, Chaudhary and her family traveled to Nepal and the United States. By example, her father instilled in her high expectations, an acceptance of taking risks, and a commitment to education. Before he died, Chaudhary's goal was to become a journalist. Since she didn't have enough money to continue her studies, Chaudhary needed to be practical and find a job immediately following her college graduation.

Seeking better opportunities than she could find in India, Chaudhary and her mother moved from India to the Washington, DC metro area. "Having relationships in journalism would have really helped in starting my career," Chaudhary lamented, but she didn't know anyone in the field.

From nouns and verbs, to debits and credits, Chaudhary decided on accounting instead of journalism and became a certified public accountant (CPA). Her first job was as an entry-level bookkeeper for an office in Washington, DC. Continuing her father's legacy of pursuing education, Chaudhary worked during the day and went to night school at Northern Virginia Community College.

Unlike other students who took one accounting class per semester, Chaudhary fast-tracked her studies and took three accounting classes at a time. Working during the day and feverishly taking classes at night, Chaudhary completed the three-year accounting curriculum in one year. She completed her course load so quickly that she needed to lobby the Washington, DC Board of Accountancy to let her sit for the CPA exam without an accounting degree and the necessary work experience. The Board of Accountancy let her sit for the CPA exam, and she passed all five sections on the first try. This is a very big deal, as the average national CPA exam pass rate is only 50 percent.

INITIAL CAREER FOCUS ON ACCOMPLISHMENTS, NOT DEVELOPING RELATIONSHIPS

Having a CPA certification opened up a key door in her career. Chaudhary landed a job at Freddie Mac, where she would ultimately work for twenty years. With determination and an accomplishment orientation, she impressed her bosses. "I was focused on getting more knowledge and experience," she said, "but I completely ignored relationships. In a large organization like Freddie Mac, I performed well in each new role and would be promoted after eighteen to twenty-four months."

Looking back, Chaudhary realized it was a mistake not to focus on relationships. "I didn't even think about how important networks and relationships really are." Chaudhary said, "I was in financial services for nearly twenty years, and at some point, I wanted to do something different." As she considered her next step in her career, Chaudhary reflects, "I didn't even know where to start. I had become so insular, focusing on excelling in the jobs that I had." She recalls, "I didn't nurture many of the people who had worked with me. Frankly, I didn't maintain those relationships."

Even though Chaudhary had not kept in touch, it was not too late. While in her career transition, she worked with a coach after Freddie Mac, who helped her realize the importance of relationships. "I never made that mistake again," she said, "Working with the coach helped me become more deliberate about relationships. The coach taught me that executive hiring decisions are often made on trusted recommendations."

SHIFTING TOWARD A KEEP-IN-TOUCH MINDSET

With her determination and work ethic, Chaudhary began her career transition project. Through trial and error, Chaudhary became disciplined in her relationship building. She got back in touch with prior colleagues and also developed relationships with new people. Her search took place before LinkedIn existed, so it took a lot of research to understand whom to speak with. "This was really hard," Chaudhary admits. "I would reach out to people and only a fraction of them would respond. I would need to follow up with people." Additionally, Chaudhary found this relationship development challenging because "I was a female who did not drink or play golf. I always made sure to have something fizzy in my glass so people would not ask any questions." While times have evolved, Chaudhary does describe a time where networking and golf went together in the C-Suite.

Her consistent outreach paid off, and she became chief financial officer of the United Way Worldwide. With a focus on relationships and keeping in touch, her career accelerated over the next fifteen years, as she became the Chief Financial Officer of *The Washington Post* as well as The Pew Charitable Trusts. She was President and Chief Operating Officer of Kettler, as well as Senior Vice President, Corporate Operations, and Chief Transformation Officer for MITRE. Currently,

Chaudhary is the Chief Operating Officer at Internews. To complement her executive roles, Chaudhary has also served on numerous nonprofit and corporate boards.

As Chaudhary's career evolved, her view on separating professional and personal relationships evolved, too. Earlier in her career, she viewed them as two distinct worlds, never to be crossed. After Freddie Mac, Chaudhary said, "I no longer separate the personal and the professional because it felt as though I was hiding something. It is really helpful to give your personal side in your work. Today, professional and personal relationships are one and the same." Chaudhary can now talk about her family, interests, volunteer activities, and hobbies even in a professional setting.

In working at *The Washington Post*, Chaudhary evolved in her approach to her relationships with her colleagues. "You can still be yourself. You can be a human being, and you can still be successful. You can make tough decisions. But you can be transparent with people, and you can show them how you feel. It doesn't all have to be your head; you can also show them insights into your heart." Over time, Chaudhary became more comfortable sharing her logic and her emotion in decision-making, which only deepened her connections to colleagues.

"GIVERS" GET BACK IN TOUCH MORE EASILY
Chaudhary has an underlying philosophy in her approach to relationships. She finds joy in helping others, which she saw her mother and father do their entire lives. "The more you give, without expecting anything in return," she declares,

"the better off you're going to be. If I make it a *quid pro quo* relationship, then it becomes a chore."

This philosophy makes Chaudhary a "giver," according to Adam Grant's book, *Give and Take: Why Helping Others Drives Our Success.* Grant defines "givers" as those who "contribute to others without seeking anything in return. They might offer assistance, share knowledge, or make valuable introductions." Chaudhary agrees. She said, "Relationships are so important, and there is a great give and take that you have. It is about helping one another. You get enriched as a result. You form friendships, and professionally, you are also helping one another become more successful."

"I've helped so many people throughout my career," Chaudhary said. "I have been a mentor to lots of people. I love helping folks with their careers. I've opened doors. I've made introductions. I've coached others. I really love it." Chaudhary recalls a specific example in which a young IT professional at Freddie Mac reached out to her with the following request: "I'm looking for a female executive to mentor me as a role model." Chaudhary replied, "Absolutely, of course." Chaudhary remembers their first meeting, which was "all about weighing whether she should stay in her current job or take a promotion that would take her slightly off her career track."

All these people she helped along the way are people she could have been keeping in touch with. Chaudhary's advice at this stage of her career, however, could not be clearer: "Start keeping in touch earlier! Since my own kids were in high school, I have been telling them relationships really matter. Take the time to get to know people. Show genuine interest in others." Most importantly, Chaudhary advises that "There is a need to be authentic. Be yourself because if you're going into a relationship, professional or personal, with a predetermined agenda, it somehow comes through. And you can tell, right? I think if you just go into it with the desire to help more than take, I think that's what creates a win-win."

YOUR RELATIONSHIP TO INFINITY TAKEAWAYS

- Networking does not come naturally to everyone – Chaudhary made relationships a priority and defined for herself how she would maintain her network.
- Reconnecting with past colleagues is an important component to nourishing your authentic social network.
- Chaudhary is a giver, and as she continued to succeed, Chaudhary continued to give back to others.
- Just Ask! – Successful people do want to hear from you and are accessible. You can ask them for help.
- The next chapter will begin to look at network theory and how you can leverage your network.

YOUR REFLECTION QUESTIONS

- Who are past colleagues and business partners you might have lost touch with?
- Would you classify yourself as a giver?
- What ways can you give to people in your network?

CHAPTER 2

Dormant Ties – Build and Rebuild Your Authentic Social Network Without the "Ick"

———

Perceptions of networking can be downright awful. The sleaze. The ask. The transaction. The superficial conversation. The uncomfortable moments. The grin-and-grab events. Is there a better way?

YOUR OWN PERCEPTIONS OF NETWORKING DEPENDS ON YOUR INTENTIONS

The word "networking" literally makes people feel dirty. Why such a visceral reaction? According to research by Gino, Casciaro, and Kouchacki, "Much too often, people confuse networking with simple extraction of value from others. Despite the clear benefits of having an extensive network, individuals often shy away from the opportunity to create new connections because engaging in instrumental networking can make them feel morally impure." Gino *et al.* examined both, "how people react to the prospect of *personal networking* in pursuit of emotional support or friendship and *instrumental networking* in pursuit of professional goals. That instrumental networking, but not personal networking, makes people feel not only anxious or inauthentic but also physically dirty. The metaphorical link between feeling morally and physically pure, or clean, is a powerful one."

Instrumental networking literally makes people feel dirty. Dove soap, anyone? Perhaps more hand sanitizer? I am a strong believer that developing a network need not make you feel sleazy or salesy though. Professionals and executives fail to distinguish between having an authentic social network and "networking" itself. An authentic social network is comprised of relationships you actually want to nourish and maintain. Understanding network theory can help bridge the gap between authentic social networks and transactional networking.

A PRIMER ON NETWORK THEORY

In the 1960s, before online social networks, the academic community began researching relationships between people. Dr. Harrison White was a trailblazer and an early network analyst. He was a key contributor to the "Harvard Revolution" in social networks, which was, at the time, an innovative approach to social interactions and personal relationships. White and his students observed society as networks rather than as large groups of individuals. White also coined the term "vacancy chain" for professional movement within a company. He found that "the careers of managers and professionals in large bureaucracies are generally contingent and form an interacting system of mobility—individual moves occur in chains of vacancies as one man replaces another."

THE STRENGTH OF WEAK TIES

Dr. Mark Granovetter, one of White's most famous students, went on to develop the seminal theory of *Strength of Weak Ties* in 1973. The *Strength of Weak Ties* is the idea that people you know casually can actually be quite helpful to you professionally. It is best known for the theory on the spread of information in social networks. Granovetter was interested in inequality as it related to the labor market. Granovetter surveyed white-collar men who landed jobs in Newton, Massachusetts and discovered the best leads for job opportunities are more likely to come from more distant acquaintances (weak ties) rather than close friends (strong ties). Granovetter learned about hydrogen bonding in his AP chemistry class in high school and the image of weak hydrogen bonds holding together huge molecules stuck with him. Granovetter was influenced by Stanley Milgram's chain letter experiment in 1967, known as the "six degrees of separation." This experiment showed that people are connected to others in their social network through a chain of acquaintances. In the experiment, people in Omaha were attempting to send a chain letter to a complete stranger in Boston. People who sent letters only to close friends never reached the stockbroker in Boston. People who sent their letters to acquaintances reached the stockbroker in Boston, changing hands around six times. The *Strength of Weak Ties* has been cited sixty-thousand-plus times (per Google Scholar) in other academic works and periodicals.

THE VALUE OF DORMANT TIES

Building on Granovetter's concept of tie strength, Professors Levin, Walter, and Murnighan wrote a paper in 2011 titled "Dormant Ties: The Value of Reconnecting." Their research asked Executive Master of Business Administration (MBA) students to consult their dormant contacts about an important work project. Their study introduces the concept of the dormant tie, "a relationship between individuals who have not communicated with each other for a long time (three years), e.g., who have drifted apart because of job mobility, divergent interests or other time demands." The professors noted that "some dormant ties used to be strong and some used to be weak."

Levin *et al.* also identify four stages in the life cycle of professional relationships: 1) formation, 2) maintenance, 3) dormancy, and 4) reconnection. Their research concluded that "reconnecting can provide substantial benefits for knowledge seekers, providing novel knowledge and insights. Reconnected ties were not dead: instead, they were both efficient and effective in providing useful knowledge." Important for those of us reconnecting with people with whom we have lost touch, Levin *et al.* offer the reassurance that "an individual's social networks have a time dimension, even a memory: past relations can be reactivated and provide efficient access to potentially critical knowledge and other resources."

	Current Ties	Dormant Ties
Strong Ties	People with whom you have a tight relationship, and with whom you are actively in touch	People with whom you had a close relationship, and with whom you have lost touch
Weak Ties	Acquaintances with whom you are in touch	Acquaintances with whom you have lost touch

CASE STUDY IN MAINTAINING AUTHENTIC RELATIONSHIPS

Academic research proves keeping in touch is a great use of your time, and it is possible to get back in touch with anyone, regardless of the tie strength. How does this relationship-nourishing activity actually work in practice, though? If anyone is committed to maintaining ties, it is Everett Hutt. He was educated in America but spent most of his professional life living and working in France. He has important perspectives on how to maintain authentic ties within your network. Currently, he is the Chief Operating Officer at Salesforce for Southern Europe, the Middle East, and Africa, but his keep-in-touch philosophy has evolved over the course of his career.

As a core principle, Hutt is against *quid pro quo* (this for that) networking and is sensitive to others' perspectives. "Hard networking and hard *quid pro quo* do not work," he says, "Nobody likes to feel like they're being abused." Like Usha Chaudhary in Chapter 1, Hutt is also a "giver" and believes interactions should "feel like a friendship." Hutt is deeply committed to investing time to remain in touch with his network and frequently catches up with classmates (*e.g.,* from high school, college, and graduate school), as well as former colleagues, supervisors, and clients. Frequently thinking of others, he is generous in providing encouragement, career ideas and sharing job leads within his network.

Hutt was, perhaps, destined to be someone who kept in touch. Before Hutt was born, his father, at the age of thirty-four, lost his brother, father, and godmother within a three-month time frame. Following these tragedies, his father had a clear outlook on relationships. Hutt recalls, "My dad would explain to me there is nothing more important than connections to your family and friends. You never know when they can fall apart."

Complementing Hutt's father, his mother equally emphasized keeping in touch. "My mother has always been a very good friend to all of our family members," he said. "My parents, from very different angles, have always stressed the importance of keeping long-term friendships." Hutt said his parents often reminded him that "it's a lot easier to keep a friend than it is to make a new friend."

REKINDLING MY OWN DORMANT TIES

In my own life and career, I have personally experienced the value of reconnection, the power of dormant and weak ties, and the importance of having a strong, authentic social network. I find joy in reconnecting with people and showing appreciation for what they have done for me. After delivering a talk, I often reach out to my college public speaking professor from Rowan University, Dr. William Kushner, to let him know I was thinking of him. From time to time, I reach out to one of my managers from Andersen Consulting (now Accenture) simply to check in and show appreciation for their early interest in my career. I don't approach them with an ask; I just show them I have not forgotten their contribution.

I have also personally benefited from the kindness of my dormant ties. In 2008, I was between jobs, having left Unilever and New York City, to be with my lovely girlfriend (now wife) in Washington, DC. To my surprise, I received an email from Mary Ann Licamele, who worked at the Career Services Office of the Georgetown MBA program. It had probably been a year since Licamele and I had spoken, but we had a great working rapport and she invited me to her office out of the blue. During our conversation, Licamele said, "Jason, how would you like to work for the career services office, part-time? We remember how helpful you were to the MBA students when you were a student. I think you should coach for us." She called me a "coach." Until that moment, I was simply helping friends, and friends of friends, find jobs for free. Not only did I receive a part-time position, but she helped me reimagine how I thought of my skills and abilities.

In the same year, I received another opportunity through another dormant tie. John Flato was the former Director of the Georgetown MBA Career Services Office. He set up a boutique consulting firm focused on campus recruiting best practices. Flato reached out with the following message: "Jason, I thought of you. Our consulting firm is being acquired by vault.com, the career website. Vault.com is expanding, and they want a presence in the Washington, DC market. They will need someone to lead a remote sales team. Why don't you talk with them?" At the time, I was not thinking about taking on a sales management role. However, Flato was persuasive and was kind enough to make the introduction to vault.com's senior management team. I was hired and remain grateful for the opportunity. Both Flato and Licamele made important contributions to my career. Because of their genuine interest in me, I gained new experiences, which eventually led to my current work today.

Remember you already have an authentic social network. Your dormant ties are waiting to hear from you. Some people have interacted with you and know your character, capabilities, and talents. You simply need to start the reconnection process. Your action step is to begin thinking about people you have already interacted with. Think about your relationships, both current and dormant, strong and weak.

YOUR RELATIONSHIP TO INFINITY TAKEAWAYS
- Networks are critical to your success.
- "Networking" does not have to be sleazy because you can have a genuine interest in people in your network.
- The "Strength of Weak Ties" principle states that acquaintances can be disproportionately helpful in your career.
- Dormant ties are an important component of your authentic social network.
- The next chapter will provide a new way for you to think about building trust in your relationships.

YOUR REFLECTION QUESTIONS

- List the individuals with whom you could potentially reconnect:
  - Dormant, strong ties
  - Dormant, weak ties
  - Current, strong ties
  - Current, weak ties

CHAPTER 3

Building Trust – Are You an Energizer?

If keeping in touch is the fuel to your relationship vehicle, then trust is the GPS that gets you there. Jeremy Butler, a Navy veteran and CEO of the Iraq and Afghanistan Veterans Association (IAVA), often thinks about trust in his nonprofit work. Funding is critical to the organization, and fundraising is often top of mind. Jeremy is intentional about taking a personal networking approach to his daily interactions. "As CEO, I am constantly getting introduced to people who are veterans at different organizations," explains Butler, "I make the time to learn about them and what they do."

Butler does not make snap judgments about whether these introductions will help his fundraising numbers. For him, getting to know people is a priority, and he makes the times in his calendar. "I think it's incredibly important," says Butler, "I believe that you can potentially learn from anyone."

EARNING TRUST IS A MULTILAYERED PROCESS

A potential client has a decision to make about which law firm to hire. A hiring committee has a decision to make about who will be their next Chief Financial Officer. Beyond experience and expertise, decisions often get made based on trust. How do you define trust, though? How do you gain someone's trust?

In *Network Drivers of Success,* Carboni, Cross, Page, and Parker observe two forms of trust in relationships: competence-based and benevolence-based trust. They assert that "both are foundational to innovation and effective collaboration."

- **Benevolence-Based Trust** – This type of trust shows you have another person's interests in mind. Without benevolence-based trust, people are reluctant to put forth and debate new or different ideas and perspectives.
- **Competence-Based Trust** – This type of trust shows you will do what you say. Without competence-based trust, people don't value the insights they receive and so don't bother to share their ideas.

In addition to defining these two types of trust, the authors highlight the special ability of "energizers" to build trust. An energizer is someone who "creates enthusiasm, in part because they engage in a set of foundational behaviors that build trust. When you interact with an energizer, you don't have to worry that you will be judged, dismissed, or devalued. Without fear of rejection, it's easier to share fledgling ideas or novel plans—to innovate, take risks, and think big."

Their research is intriguing because an "energizer" can be someone of any personality type. According to Carboni *et al.*, "Energizers win not because they are happy people—although they usually are—but because the way that they engage with others results in better opportunities, ideas, talent, and resources that flow to them over time. People want to be around energizers."

THE CHARISMA MYTH – INTROVERTS ARE EQUALLY CAPABLE OF BUILDING TRUST

It is counterintuitive, perhaps, but you may be unable to recognize an energizer immediately. Carboni *et al.* note that "energizers may not be who you think they are. Certainly, they aren't all stereotypical cheerleaders or hyper-extraverted networkers. In fact, a low-key person is just as likely to be an energizer as someone who is considered charismatic, and introverts are just as likely to be seen as energizing as extroverts." What makes someone an energizer is the capacity to listen and understand another person's perspective—someone willing to brainstorm ideas to make them better.

This research rings true for my executive clients who self-identify as introverts. They often complain they are not "people people" when in reality, their superpower is the ability to observe and listen. Whether during an executive interview for a senior-level job, or a pitch meeting for professional services work, my clients build trust by staying in the moment and asking genuine questions of the person in front of them.

PORTRAITS OF ENERGIZERS

Ann Ford, the Executive Director of Clients and Sectors for DLA Piper, a global law firm in forty-plus countries, is the quintessential "energizer." Formally trained as an intellectual property attorney, she is now a member of the firm's global board, executive committee, and firmwide policy committee. In her early attorney years, a more senior attorney advised Ford, "Your client isn't hiring you for your wisdom, intelligence, or your expertise. Your client is hiring you for peace of mind. They don't need to know how the sausage is made; they just need to know that things are going to be okay." Ford took this advice to heart and counseled, "You've got to be the trusted advisor, where the client feels confident with you. Whatever the client throws at you in your area of expertise, you need to assure them. It might not be you who has all the answers, but you'll get someone you can trust to work with them."

In building trust with her clients, Ford observes that "each client is different on the risk scale." For her, listening is essential to building trust. "It is about figuring out where they're coming from and what matters to them. This allows me to focus on delivering on what I say I'm going to do and ensure the attorneys I train are similarly going to deliver alongside me."

Chris Lu, a senior White House official under President Obama, is another "energizer." Though he certainly builds both competence and benevolence-based trust, he emphasizes the ability of kindness as a critical component of trust-building. "Be a good person," he says. "In life, you should be a good person, but especially in politics, you should be a good person. Politics is really the last great meritocracy. It's the last place where nobody cares where you went to school, or even if you graduated at all. You can rise from working in the mailroom or being a driver to becoming the chief of staff. You should be nice to everybody above, at your level, and below. In particular, your word counts for something. You should be a person of integrity and credibility. There's a lot of partisanship. There's a lot of conflict. But if you talk to Republicans I worked with on Capitol Hill, they'll say: 'I didn't always agree with this guy, but he was a person of credibility. When he said something, I could trust that his word counted for something.'" Lu's kindness and humanity energize the people he interacts with. Even if others around you aren't behaving like good people, Lu understands that being one yourself tends to get others to up their game. If you model the behavior you want to see, (some) others will follow you.

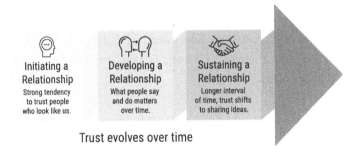

Initiating a Relationship
Strong tendency to trust people who look like us.

Developing a Relationship
What people say and do matters over time.

Sustaining a Relationship
Longer interval of time, trust shifts to sharing ideas.

Trust evolves over time

DON'T RUSH THE PROCESS BEHIND BUILDING TRUST

As Mary K Young, a Partner at Zeughauser Group, advanced in her career, she began to form opinions on trust. She firmly believes building trusted relationships happens over time. "You can't walk in the room and say, 'trust me,'" she explains. "Conversely, you can't walk in the room and trust the other person either. I believe in listening and caring about what the other person has to say. You have to deliver on your commitments. All these things build mutual trust."

One of Young's first projects as CMO of a large law firm was a massive market research project designed to determine what factors lead potential clients to trust a law firm enough to hire its attorneys. "We actually went out interviewed hundreds of buyers of legal services, including clients and non-clients, to form a baseline and learn about the purchasing journey. We studied how they buy legal services, make their decisions, their demographics, what roles they are in, who else they chose for the same work, and what they thought of some of our competitors." What did this research find? According to Young, the two key factors buyers of legal services relied on in making purchasing decisions were relationships and understanding the client's business. She said, "Often, we would need to get attorneys to stop talking about themselves and begin to ask questions of their clients. Listening on both sides of the table increased trust over time."

Phil de Picciotto also believes trust-building can't be rushed. De Picciotto is the Founder and President of Octagon, where he has been at the forefront of the sports, music, and entertainment industry for more than thirty-five years. He is responsible for the global operations of Octagon's worldwide talent representation, property representation and ownership, event management, and financial wealth management businesses. He oversees Octagon's client portfolio of more than one thousand of the world's most high-profile and accomplished personalities. Their incredible client roster includes Michael Phelps, Giannis Antetokounmpo,

Simone Biles, Stephen Curry, Elena Delle Donne, Gary Player, Jimmie Johnson, Gleybar Torres, Jeanette Lee, and Leon Draisaitl.

"For me," says de Picciotto, "the formula is simple. To have a chance of forming a lasting business relationship, you have to get to know someone, and they have to get to know you. Once you get to know people, you can decide if you like them. People do business with each other largely based on liking them, when the services, costs, and timing are the same. Some people want to be trusted right at the very beginning. But frankly, I think they are rushing a process that really can't be rushed." According to de Picciotto, "trust is the glue. Meeting people is the opportunity. Liking people is optimizing. Trusting is gluing that optimization for the long term."

De Picciotto also sees trust as a commitment to oneself. "If you don't trust yourself," he says, "you're not going to trust other people." What is the best way to learn to trust yourself? De Picciotto says it is to avoid violating your own values and principles. "Don't do things that you know are not right or not fair. If you can sleep well at night, then I think you will experience very few erosions of trust with other people."

Jeremy Butler, Ann Ford, Chris Lu, Mary K Young, and Phil de Picciotto have different professions and backgrounds. What unites them is their authentic approach to building trust. As they continue to care about other people's perspectives, they continually earn the trust of their stakeholders.

YOUR RELATIONSHIP TO INFINITY TAKEAWAYS

- Trust is critical to relationship-building.
- Competence-based trust is about making sure people know you will do what you say. Benevolence-based trust is about showing you care about people's interests.
- Energizers build trust because they help people feel comfortable sharing ideas without harsh judgment or retribution.
- Don't fall into the "I need to be charismatic" trap. Energizers who build trust can come in any personality type.
- Trust building takes time. There's no need to rush the process.
- Listening is a key part of building trust.
- Next up chapter will help you think through how to get beyond your "Social Fortress."

YOUR REFLECTION QUESTIONS

- Who are the energizers in your network?
- What might you experiment with to become an energizer in your relationships?
- Have you tried to rush trust in a relationship? What happened as a result?
- If you are an extrovert, how do you slow yourself down so you can listen better?

CHAPTER 4

Addressing Your "Social Fortress" – You Actually Know More People Than You Think

———

I am sitting with my client "Eric" at his computer. He looks at the empty email with hesitation. He knows he needs to write something. We have spent several sessions identifying people he could reach out to. In our conversations, Eric was reminded of a law school classmate whom he had not spoken to in ten years. Eric's career took him into public service, and his friend moved up the ranks in-house at a *Fortune* 500 company. Admittedly, Eric has lost touch. Eric decided to leave public service, and his law school friend is actually working at a company with a job opening Eric is interested in.

Getting back in touch with your dormant ties (*e.g.,* old friends, classmates, colleagues, and acquaintances) can seem overwhelming. It can be hard to know where to begin. A talented attorney makes partner and wants advice on how to go about bringing in clients. A tenured executive at a government contractor might be asked to retire as part of a succession plan. In any of these scenarios, the individuals involved would likely benefit from exploring ideas with others about their options, choices, and potential next steps.

My clients often ask questions such as, "Who could I possibly reach out to?" "What would I say?" and "Would they really take my call?" These executives, who led successful careers over twenty, thirty, or forty years, struggle even to identify an initial list of ten people they might reach out to.

UNDERSTANDING THE SOCIAL FORTRESS

In "Status Differences in the Cognitive Activation of Social Networks," Smith, Menon, and Thompson observe that "although people often winnow their networks in times of threat, several lines of research suggest that expanding one's social network might be the optimal response. The social fortress of one's close, trusted friends and family is a comfortable refuge but also offers fewer pathways to escape the threat. Broad, non-dense networks, by comparison, provide less in terms of sympathy but may allow people to emerge relatively unscathed from job loss by increasing access to employment-related information." I agree that the image of a "social fortress" is a self-imposed illusion. Walls exist in our minds regarding the myriad of people who actually form our available network.

IDENTIFYING PEOPLE TO REACH OUT TO – YOUR POTENTIAL NETWORK

To identify people for an outreach list, I always stress to my clients the importance of thinking broadly. Smith *et al.* define a "potential network" as the full set of contacts people have at their disposal. Within the potential network, they further define a concept called the "activated network," which is "nested within the potential network, i.e., the subset of the potential network that actually comes to mind in a given situation." What I have always found fascinating in this stage is the self-imposed wall talented people create for themselves. They do not fully see their "potential network."

Smith *et al.* further assert, "The concept of the activated network draws from past research contending that social networks are more than realized, objective social structures: they are also cognitive structures. People might fail to remember particular contacts, be unable to recognize their value, or mentally reject contacts because they feel apprehensive about calling on them."

The self-imposed "Social Fortress" is a real barrier to reconnection. My clients commonly identify a person and then reject them immediately, saying, "That person works in finance in that organization, but I am looking for a senior role in operations. They won't be able to help." A false boundary is created, while my client ignores an important fact: the person in finance likely has developed a broad network within their own organization to be successful. The person in finance probably has created a level of trust in the organization and understands its internal ways of working. For my client, reaching out creates an opportunity to access knowledge beyond what would be found on the company's website and job posting. If only they would send the email.

Another real struggle in mapping a potential network is the genuine failure of memory. LinkedIn can be a great resource in jogging people's memory about who they actually know. Chapter 9 will address how to use LinkedIn to authentically keep in touch.

REACHING OUT – MOBILIZING YOUR POTENTIAL NETWORK

Once you have identified your potential network, the next step is to start reaching out. Smith *et al.* describe a "mobilized network," which consists of "the subset of the activated network that people actually solicit resources from when they engage in help-seeking behaviors. Whereas the activated network involves a private mental activity that logically precedes mobilization, mobilization is a social activity through which people call on contacts and seek resources from them." How you reach out is up to you, and you have a wide array of media you can use to communicate with your network, even if you are not in the same city or time zone as they are. You have available to you a veritable communication buffet: email, text, direct message, phone, holiday cards, and letters. All are easy ways to say hello or ask for some time.

Also, remember you need not reach out to every single individual in your network. As Simon *et al.* assert, "Certain situational triggers (*e.g.,* job loss) may prompt people to activate different aspects of their networks. Individual social networks, therefore, are temporally dynamic over the long run (*i.e.,* the composition of the potential network shifts gradually over time)." In other words, people come in and out of your life.

CLIENT CASE STUDY ON TEARING DOWN A SOCIAL FORTRESS

All of us have some form of a social fortress in our heads. Some fortresses are just bigger than others. "Mark," a litigator and senior partner at an *AmLaw* 100 law firm, reached out to me about his retirement strategy. Mark went to a top undergraduate university and top law school and had a successful legal career. Additionally, he was a serial nonprofit board member and was active in his law firm's *pro bono* efforts. After thirty-five years in practice, Mark knew it was time for a change. He was based in Washington, DC, but he wanted to move closer to his aging father in the southern part of the United States.

After doing some initial work on identifying his interests, we began work on turning Mark's retirement transition ideas into reality. Having sat on many nonprofit boards, Mark sought either a general counsel (GC) or chief operating officer role within a nonprofit organization. As a Methodist, he also considered opportunities to leverage his legal and governance skill set in church administration.

As we discussed his options, I stressed the importance of his current relationships and reconnecting with them. As our sessions progressed, I encouraged Mark to list out people he already knew and with whom he could initiate conversations. Some of these were people he had kept in touch with, and some were people with whom he had lost touch. When we finally developed the list, it reflected aspects of both his private practice and nonprofit service.

From my vantage point, Mark was well-positioned to find an opportunity quickly. I thought to myself, "Wow. He has so much to work with. He had so many interesting and trusted relationships." Mark was a giver by nature and took a real interest in people over the years. However, for Mark, reconnecting was complex and difficult. While he was at ease giving, Mark had rarely asked for help before. Additionally, Mark was an introvert and was never truly comfortable with chitchat and small talk. Mark was stuck.

To keep his search moving, we developed a micro plan. During one session, we would identify five people to reach out to via email. Mark would then email them for a conversation while I sat with him. The first three people he identified were the lowest-hanging fruit. Even though he had been out of touch for about six months, he knew these people would be helpful. By the end of our session, two of the three had already responded and we were off to the races. Each week, it became easier for Mark to have conversations with more of the people he had worked with. To Mark's surprise, people with whom he had lost touch (ten, fifteen, or even twenty-plus years ago) were happy to hear from him and help him in his transition.

Most importantly, Mark recognized how much people valued his insights, strategic guidance, and mentor and leadership abilities. As he progressed with each conversation, two important things happened: 1) Mark's memory of people in his network (*e.g.*, alumni of his law firm, former law school classmates, peer Board members of nonprofits) increased;

and 2) He actually became more excited about contacting these people. He went beyond his social fortress to a snowball of reconnections and positive interactions. The entire process of connecting with fifty-plus people rekindled his confidence and his own trust in his abilities. After fifteen months of these structured conversations, he found a GC role in church administration. He continued to keep in touch with these people afterward.

KEEPING THE SOCIAL FORTRESS AT BAY

Self-described introvert Kevin DeSanto also evolved in how he thinks about connecting and reconnecting with others. DeSanto is Managing Director and cofounder of KippsDeSanto, an investment bank and wholly owned subsidiary of Capital One since 2019. He grew up in Central Pennsylvania, in a house where people didn't really talk about career aspirations or professional relationships. "You were expected to work hard, get good grades, and get a job," DeSanto explains, "We didn't talk about business. I didn't get on an airplane until I was a freshman in college. It was a regular small-town experience."

DeSanto could have let a social fortress surround him. However, he decided to get out of his comfort zone as he grew up. DeSanto said the idea of developing relationships "just sort of grew on me as I went through college and then into the workforce." He reflects on what playing college baseball at Georgetown University did for him. "Being an athlete, I was always around teams. Professionally, I wanted a similar connection to people." DeSanto reflects, "I sought out relationships one at a time."

"I know I am introverted," DeSanto explains, "so I need to push myself. The competitive dynamics of having played sports and the experience of having some level of success have helped me." In terms of reaching out and staying connected, DeSanto describes his approach as a "flywheel," quite the opposite of a "social fortress." "Lawyers, bankers, consultants, past clients, and government officials all form some of the dozens of spokes on the flywheel," he says. "In my business, my colleagues and I also have to stay pretty actively engaged with buyers and investors, and people who are on the other side of the transactions from us. We have to do a good job of staying in contact and try to keep in touch with them. I try to find opportunities or send referrals to stay top of mind. It's about adding value to that flywheel, just as much as we possibly can."

DeSanto sees relationship development as a daily habit. "It is not just putting a block on your calendar for Friday to network. It's just always happening. You never know when something's going to lead to something." DeSanto acknowledges that "you can't stay in touch with everybody for decades on a day-to-day or monthly basis. You just need to do enough to stay on the radar."

Both Mark and DeSanto would admit their instinct is to build a social fortress and not reach out. But both leaders have pushed through their resistance and found an opportunity on the other side. By making an effort to activate his relationship base, Mark made a successful retirement transition. Similarly, DeSanto treats relationship development as a daily activity, which has allowed him and his firm to succeed.

YOUR RELATIONSHIP TO INFINITY TAKEAWAYS

- A "social fortress" can prevent us from identifying and reaching out to our full network.
- Many people struggle to identify all the members of their network.
- Reaching out and connecting with people actually prompts people to remember others they know.
- You do not need to reach out to every person in your network.
- The next chapter reviews the importance of friendships in connection and reconnection.

YOUR REFLECTION QUESTIONS

- Have you ever retreated to your own "social fortress" at a time when you needed help?
- If so, what actions might break down your fortress?
- Do you have a flywheel? Into what categories would you put the people on your flywheel?
- This list might help you get started:
  - Friends
  - Family
  - Colleagues
  - Clients
  - Prospective Clients
  - Business Partners
  - High school, College and Graduate School Classmates
- To get started, identify one or two people in each category.

CHAPTER 5

Make the Time – The Social Science Behind Friendships

___

A chapter on friendships in a business-related book? Seriously? This was not a topic I expected to cover here in any detail. However, it turns out the social science behind friendships is directly related to career growth. After conducting twenty-plus interviews for this book and reviewing articles and academic research, it became clear that friendships are the underlying form of connection for relationships – both personal *and* professional. The COVID-19 pandemic has only amplified our need for human interaction and connection, too.

OUR BRAINS ARE WIRED FOR SOCIAL THINKING

In *Scientific American*, "Why We are Wired to Connect," psychologist Matthew Lieberman asserts, "Our need to connect with other people is even more fundamental, more basic, than our need for food or shelter." Our brains are actually trained to think about people. Liberman and his team conducted functional magnetic imaging (fMRI) research at their UCLA lab. They concluded, "There are two distinct networks that support social and non-social thinking and that as one network increases its activity, the other tends to quiet down – kind of like a neural seesaw. Whenever we finish doing some kind of non-social thinking, the network for social thinking comes back on like a reflex – almost instantly."

"Why would the brain be set up to do this?" Liberman wondered. "We have recently found that this reflex prepares us to walk into the next moment of our lives focused on the minds behind the actions that we see from others. Evolution has placed a bet that the best thing for our brain to do in any spare moment is to get ready to see the world socially. I think that makes a major statement about the extent to which we are built to be social creatures." Social science research has concluded we are hardwired to be social creatures. Introvert or extrovert. Young or old. Building connection is at our very core.

RECIPROCITY IS AN IMPORTANT COMPONENT OF FRIENDSHIP

Yes, we are hardwired for social connection, but it takes more than that to form a friendship. It also takes reciprocity. In *Psychology Today*, "The Most Important Element of Any Friendship," Suzanne Degges-White, PhD, writes, "True friendships are measured by the presence of reciprocity in the relationship, meaning that both individuals consider the other to be a friend. It's like those well-liked people in the office or on the playground whom everyone considers a friend because they can make everyone feel appreciated or welcome. If that popular person is asked to list her friends, however, she may only name a handful of good friends, whereas dozens of others might claim *her* as a friend. Or think about the less-well-liked people you work with—they may have no colleague who'd "claim" them as a friend, even if they can generate a long list of people *they* consider friends. Without reciprocity, friendships just don't exist."

What about social media connections as "friendships"? Degges-White reflects on the need for reciprocity in the online world, too. "Today, many people measure their worth and popularity by their number of 'followers,' 'friends,' and 'connections' on social media platforms," she writes. "It's almost like Nielsen ratings for people. Of course, while a character like Hodor from *Game of Thrones* has become a welcome guest in millions of homes on Sunday nights, no one could expect Hodor to reciprocate the familiarity." She concludes that "friendships begin with *reciprocity,* but to truly flourish they require loyalty, empathetic concern, honesty, thoughtfulness, connection, and trust. Reciprocity is the starting point, but it takes more than that to make it last."

HOW MUCH TIME DOES IT *REALLY* TAKE TO BUILD A FRIENDSHIP?

In addition to reciprocity, time plays an integral role in how we develop friendships. In the *Journal of Social and Personal Relationships*, "How many hours does it take to make a friend?" Dr. Jeffrey Hall uncovered, "the time spent together was associated with closer friendships." In his research, Hall was looking for cutoff points, identifying "a 50 percent greater likelihood you switch from acquaintance to casual friend and from casual friend to friend, then again from friend to a close friend." He found it took:

- Fifty hours of interaction to move from acquaintance to casual friend
- Ninety hours to move from casual friend to friend
- Two-hundred-plus hours to qualify as a best friend

Since most of our week is spent at work, it makes sense to spend that time forming friendships with colleagues, vendors, clients, and business partners. Whether you work a forty- or sixty-hour work week, frequently interacting can allow your colleagues to move from casual friend, to friend, to best friend.

The conclusions Hall draws from this work are straightforward but important. "You have to invest," he advises. "Decades of research have shown that friendship is not just one of life's pleasures; it's one of life's necessities. Having friends helps to keep us healthy, both physically and mentally. On the other hand, a lack of social connectedness is as bad for us as smoking or obesity. Yet we don't always budget our time accordingly," says Hall. "It's clear that many adults don't feel they have a lot of time, but these relationships are not going to develop just by wanting them. You have to prioritize time with people."

Barbara McDuffie, a business development executive for the national accounting firm, Baker Tilly, understands the value of spending the time to deepen relationships. "I like to keep in touch with people because I care," she says. She recalls a specific situation where a large client in Florida called her with a request. Her client asked, "I am so appreciative of how you kept in touch with us. You have become, like a friend. By the way, will you help my son get a job?" McDuffie laughed, "I told my client I would find something for his son because I valued the time we spent together."

HOW TO "FIND" THE TIME FOR FRIENDSHIPS

We know friendships are necessary for our well-being, and it takes time to build and nourish these relationships. In turning ideas into action, though, the real challenge is finding the time.

For advice on time-management subjects, my wife and I often turn to the work of Laura Vanderkam, author of *168 Hours: You Have More Time Than You Think*. Vanderkam writes that "if something is important to you, you simply have to put it in your schedule first." She further explains that "to 'align your time' is to build in time for friendships by including friends in your regular activities. I try to meet friends for lunch sometimes – I have to eat anyway, and this is usually a time when I have childcare. Or we have friends who don't have the babysitter problem over for a late dinner...And over the years, I've actually found it easiest to keep up friendships with people who also sing in my choir, the Young New Yorkers' Chorus. We rehearse every Tuesday night, so it's pretty easy to grab a drink afterward or socialize during our breaks."

Julissa Marenco agrees with Vanderkam's philosophy. She is currently the Assistant Secretary, Office of Communications and External Affairs and Chief Marketing Officer for the

Smithsonian Institution, the world's largest museum, education, and research complex. "You need to remember to ping people for no reason whatsoever." Right before our interview, Marenco told me she had scheduled time to call two friends "out of the blue." "I had two conversations with them for five to ten minutes. We were all happy to hear from each other," she said. "I do a lot of spontaneous calling, which I don't think is the norm these days."

Personally, I love Vanderkam's guidance about identifying priorities and integrating your activities to advance your friendships and Marenco's intentional but spontaneous outreach. I have been guilty of going down rabbit holes of watching TV or browsing social media rather than spending time nurturing friendships. During COVID-19, however, I took ownership over keeping in touch with my friends, just as I do with my professional relationships.

Some of my friends have moved and live in different time zones, both domestically and internationally. To kickstart the getting back-in-touch process with my friends, I started writing down the names of each friend I wanted to reconnect with. I then decided each month to reach out to at least one friend and get back in touch. By the end of my first year, I had gotten back in touch with twelve friends. It took some scheduling and rescheduling. Some people were available to chat during the day, while others could talk only at night or on weekends. All were happy to hear from me, and I was hooked.

Simply setting and acting on a monthly friend intention allowed me to reconnect with people from high school, college, and business school. I had also connected with friends from prior work experiences. There was no ask; I just wanted to see how people were doing.

Through this reconnection process, I realized I am a social animal in need of connection. Am I done? Not at all. That is what *Relationships to Infinity* is all about. I continue to update my lists so I can connect and reconnect.

YOUR RELATIONSHIP TO INFINITY TAKEAWAYS

- Our minds are actually wired for social interaction.
- Friendship is critical to our social and emotional well-being.
- Friendship requires reciprocity.
- Building a casual friendship takes fifty hours; moving from casual friendship to friendship takes ninety hours; and it takes an additional two hundred hours to qualify as a best friend.
- Prioritizing time on your calendar for these friendships is critical to maintaining them.
- The next chapter will help you break through your own Bermuda "Keep-in-Touch" Triangle.

YOUR REFLECTION QUESTIONS

- Are you currently blocking time for your friends?
- On a monthly basis, how much time are you committing to your friendships?
- If you were to catch up with one friend in the next month, who would it be?
- If you are primarily working remotely, how can you make time to keep in touch with your work friends?

CHAPTER 6

Moving Beyond the Bermuda Keep-in-Touch Triangle

———

In the legend of the Bermuda Triangle, ships and aircraft enter its space, never to be seen again. When it comes to keeping in touch with their networks, I have witnessed my own clients' intentions vanish without a trace. In Chapter 4, we learned your "social fortress" can limit your interactions to a small group of people. While the fortress might help you feel safe and comfortable, this career-limiting behavior reduces your access to a broader network. What exactly are the barriers to connecting and keeping in touch with that broader network, and how can we break them down? Barriers to connection and reconnection can be both self-imposed and societal.

I am not a therapist. However, in my ten years of coaching executives, I have observed a great deal of worry, fear, and guilt when my clients are asked to connect or reconnect with members of their network. They tell me endless stories of all the reasons why someone would NOT want to talk with them. NOT want to help them. They share the guilt they feel about not having done a good job of keeping in touch and not being worthy of a favor. They are crushed by the fear that it might NOT work or they could look weak or silly. When this fear, worry, and guilt combine, I believe my clients enter their personal "Bermuda keep-in-touch triangle."

UNDERSTANDING OUR OWN BERMUDA TRIANGLE

Brian Peters, EdD, a Senior Human Capital Consultant at Franklin IQ, has a Doctorate in Counseling Psychology from George Washington University. He agrees that worry, fear, and guilt limit our ability to interact, connect and reconnect with people. Dr. Peters explained these three emotions to me when we spoke:

- **Worry – "Worry is a normal human defense mechanism.** The limbic system in our brain is the emotional part of our brain and houses the amygdala. The amygdala can cause the flight response so that long ago, we would run away from bears. In modern-day life, we worry about getting our work done before the day ends. We worry about whether we are going to be entertaining enough at a party. But if worry prevents us from going to a party, or prevents us from calling our friends, then that becomes anxiety, which is natural. In terms of connecting and reconnecting, some level of anxiety is good because it gets us to put a little more effort into the email and actually care what we're saying to someone."

- **Fear** – "**Fear, like worry, is a normal emotional response, which lives on a continuum.** I fear this will not work out. I fear the person will not respond to my message. I fear the person is going to take this the wrong way, and I will look bad. I fear that I will lose this friend, and then I will be alone and homeless, etc. Fear is worry that has escalated."
- **Guilt** – "**Guilt is a feeling of shame or regret.** When it comes to having not called someone in five or ten years, guilt is a normal thing. You might have had things going on in your life and just lost touch. It a normal human emotion to feel guilty for not having kept in touch."

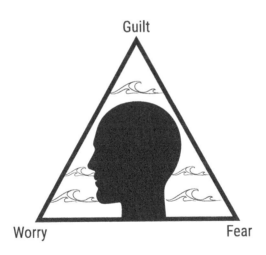

ANYONE CAN BREAK FREE FROM THE BERMUDA KEEP-IN-TOUCH TRIANGLE

Dr. Peters is emphatic on the following point: "Extrovert or introvert, you still need interpersonal connections." Peters describes personal relationships as a "protective factor" that shields us from a number of evils. "Whether you're an extrovert or an introvert," he says, "you can have equally good social connections as a protective factor against things such as worry, fear, and guilt, as well as against anxiety, depression, and just about every other negative aspect of mental health. You may be more tired or less tired after interacting, depending on whether you are an introvert or extrovert, but you still need those connections." Dr. Peters also believes in the following three strategies for overcoming worry, fear, and guilt that can come with connection and reconnection:

- **Create an Optimistic Internal Narrative** – "Optimism is going to lead toward better connections. Psychological resilience is important in having a high protective factor. The goal is to create a positive internal story to anticipate a favorable result."
- **Set Goals That Form Habits** – "Mini-quantitative goals will be helpful in starting a reconnecting habit. For example, write an email once a week or once a month to someone with whom you have lost touch. These small, measurable goals can help form habits."
- **Write Down the Most Likely Scenario** – "Journaling is healthy in general because it helps you process feelings and information in a logical way. Journaling moves you away from your emotional response. It is healthy to write down what you believe will be the most likely response from the person you are reaching out to, which will encourage action."

SOCIETAL BARRIERS TO KEEPING IN TOUCH

Not all barriers to keeping in touch are self-imposed. In my work as a coach, I have also observed societal barriers to keeping in touch, particularly for people who are in minority groups. To better understand these issues, I reached out to Stacy Blake-Beard, PhD, an expert on leadership, mentoring, inclusion, and diversity. Dr. Blake-Beard is currently a professor at the Tuck School of Business at Dartmouth and served as the 2016–2019 Deloitte Ellen Gabriel Chair of Women and Leadership at the Simmons College School of Business, where she taught organizational leadership. Previously, Blake-Beard was also on the faculty at the Harvard University Graduate School of Education for six years. Earlier in her career, she worked in sales and marketing at Procter & Gamble and in the corporate human resources department at Xerox.

"I am very interested in intersectionality in how we show up in different identities – gender, race, economic status, and sexual orientation," says Dr. Blake-Beard. These identities affect relationship-building. Dr. Blake-Beard observes that "people connect with each other through similarity or attraction. For example, if I am similar to you, then I am attracted to you. It becomes much easier to build a connection. As a black woman, I need to figure out commonality with someone else, beyond race or gender. For example, I might need to initiate conversations about travel, pets, or sports. People in the minority need to take an extra step in order to build connection."

Once you find that level of similarity, though, Dr. Blake-Beard says, "Your differences become less important. It is detective work to figure out what dimensions are important and how we connect. From there, it is about figuring out how to communicate your need for help, as well as showing you can help the other person too."

"The biggest issue for women and people of color," Dr. Blake-Beard observes, "is that when you ask for help, your competency is questioned. Your capabilities are doubted. Asking for help makes you appear vulnerable. These barriers become a wall that prevents us from reaching out because we become concerned about how we are perceived. You create a shell to protect yourself, and sometimes that shell is a barrier to building relationships." These are very real, negative responses to outreach, which are barriers to reconnection.

STRONG TIES MATTER FOR PEOPLE NOT IN THE MAJORITY

The research related to strong and weak ties (see Chapter 2) also may not apply equally to people in the minority. "People who are not in the majority have to do more work in how they show up in relationships and at work," Dr. Blake-Beard notes. "With respect to network theory, they have to do more work to create the initial connection and evolve it from a weak to a strong tie. The "Strength of Weak Ties" is a classic principle, but when it comes to people who are not in the majority, weak ties might not put up social capital to help."

Dr. Blake-Beard concludes, "You need people in your network willing to put their name out for you. I believe people who are not in the majority need more strong ties than those in the majority."

CASE STUDY ON BREAKING OUT OF THE BERMUDA TRIANGLE

In practice, how can you release yourself from the worry, fear, and guilt of reconnecting and free yourself from your own Bermuda Keep-in-Touch Triangle? My client, "Linda," is a perfect example of someone who broke free.

She is the General Counsel and Ethics Officer for a public sector organization. She is a member of the storied sorority, Alpha Kappa Alpha, as well as a longstanding participant in the professional association, Corporate Counsel Women of Color (CCWC). Linda grew up in Detroit, MI, where her father was a judge, and her mother was a teacher and school counselor. On the block where she grew up, her neighbors were people of color, like her. They were locally elected officials and the chiefs of police and the fire department. Detroit also had a black mayor. Having these role models, Linda believed anything was possible for a person of color. In giving career advice, her father was clear: "You need to be on boards. You need to be in the room where decisions are made so that you can influence things." However, she admits, "Relationships were not discussed as a way to get there."

When Linda and I started working together, she had transitioned from a senior in-house counsel role at a *Fortune* 100 corporation. "I was very slow to understand the value of relationships," she reflects, "I think I was reticent about deciding who would really want to help me. 'Oh, that's too much to ask,' I would tell myself."

As Linda and I began bringing her job search strategy to life, she recognized how important it was to engage the people who wanted to help her. She had been active in her law school's alumni association at the University of Michigan. She had been an active participant with CCWC. She had past colleagues who respected her because of a very impressive career in the public and private sectors. Unfortunately, however, she created a shell for herself. She was reluctant to reach out, as her internal voice was saying, "That would be an imposition," "They don't have time for me," and her self-admitted personal motto, "I should do it myself."

As we worked on replacing these thoughts with more helpful ones, she began to reach out to people in her network. And when she did, Linda received an overwhelmingly positive response. She said, "I was surprised at how people were genuinely happy to hear from me. They liked and respected me in the same way that I did them."

In addition to her individual outreach, Linda leveraged the CCWC annual conference. She said, "At CCWC, the founder and president would encourage us to meet one another to make sure we were developing relationships. That encouragement stuck with me. This CCWC leader made it real to me that relationship building was an everyday, ongoing activity and that this should be a part of your process in your career."

The wise words of her CCWC colleagues inspired Linda to break free from her own Bermuda Keep-in-Touch Triangle. As she engaged all of her relationships, Linda landed a General Counsel role. Now in her new job, Linda continues the keep-in-touch work she started during her job search. "Now my outreach is much more intentional," she said. "I realized you can't keep all of this information about all your connections top of mind all the time. You have to be more consistent about reconnecting and then act on those intentions. It has to be genuine. Staying in touch should instead be part of your everyday life."

For Linda, this keeping in touch activity does not come naturally. "I push myself to make sure that this has become routine," she admits. "Just like you do with exercise, right?" Linda asserts, "I push myself to make sure that my mindset is open to reconnecting, which allows me to act on my keep-in-touch goals."

Linda has created a thirty-minute slot in her calendar every week to ensure she focuses on keeping in touch. She gave this activity a name: "CC" or "Connection Calls." "The point is to make it top of mind," she says, "Because work never stops. It would be really easy to let the week go, let two weeks go and not do any of this. So it literally is a calendar entry; that's my intentionality."

"I am still an introvert who presents like an extrovert," Linda admits. She's an introvert with important wisdom to share for others who, like her, may not be in the majority, though. "People of color should not saddle themselves with the idea that they are not deserving of other people's time or that it's too much of an imposition for them to reach out."

YOUR RELATIONSHIP TO INFINITY TAKEAWAYS

- Fear, worry, and guilt can create a self-imposed Bermuda Keep-In-Touch Triangle.
- Introverts and extroverts can create a high protective factor through positive social connections.
- Journaling and goal setting are ways to reduce fear, worry, and guilt around connecting and reconnecting.
- People who are not in the majority need to rely on strong tie relationships.
- Linda showed she could break free from her own Bermuda "Keep-in-Touch" Triangle.
- The next chapter will provide research-based ways to actually get back in touch.

YOUR REFLECTION QUESTIONS

- Based on the list you created from Chapter 4, do you have any fear, worry, or guilt about reaching out to these individuals?
- Journal about the most likely scenario of what will happen when you reach out to them. What did you discover through this journaling exercise?
- Do you have a "Connection Call" set on your calendar this week? This month?

CHAPTER 7

What Is the "Right" Way to Reconnect?

Congratulations! You escaped your Bermuda Keep-In-Touch Triangle and are charting a course toward solid relationship reconnection habits. As you get ready to reconnect, you may be wondering about the medium and format of reconnection. My clients often ask, "how exactly do I do this? Via Text? E-mail? Smoke signal? Carrier pigeon? Is there really a right way to reconnect?" While no approach is "perfect," here are some criteria to consider before you begin reaching out.

COMMUNICATE SO THERE IS NO URGENCY

Assuming you are taking a genuine approach to reconnecting, pick a communication medium that does not rush the other person. In her *New York Times* piece, "Should You Reach Out to a Former Friend Right Now?" Ann Goldfarb advises that "email or direct messages over social media is a good place to reestablish contact. This way, your former friend can read your message in private and decide how they want to respond." You never know what a person is going through, so I wholeheartedly agree with Goldfarb's approach. Depending on your relationship with the person and how long it has been since you have been in touch, you might also consider writing a letter or postcard. A little personalization goes a long way.

GRATITUDE HELPS TOO

My parents always taught me to say "please" and "thank you." As a child, they got me into the habit of writing thank you notes for birthday, Bar Mitzvah, and Hanukkah gifts. As I became a professional, I purchased my own stationery and started writing thank you notes to mentors and people who helped me along the way. It turns out thanking people is actually a very big deal!

Professors Francesca Gino and Adam Grant have studied the power of gratitude. In "A Little Thanks Goes a Long Way: Explaining Why Gratitude Expressions Motivate Prosocial Behavior," they explain that "when helpers are thanked for their efforts, the resulting sense of being socially valued, more than the feelings of competence they experience, are critical in encouraging them to provide more help in the future." In thanking those who have supported you, not only are you showing genuine appreciation for their generosity, but you are also encouraging future assistance.

LEAD WITH POSITIVE MEMORIES OF THE PERSON – NOSTALGIA WORKS

In my work with executive clients, we talk through possible ways of reconnecting with former clients, colleagues, and friends. The question I hear most often is, "What do I say?" My response is, "It is not what you say, but what you remember about them." You may have just listened to a song a former colleague sang all the time that reminded you of that person. You might have received a nice win at work, and you are reminded of a past supervisor who helped you along the way. You have likely learned skills from prior colleagues, supervisors, classmates, vendors, and business partners, which you continue to use today.

Sadhvi Subramanian, formerly a Senior Vice President at Capital One, is an excellent example of someone who remembers those who have helped her along the way. She says, "If someone I have asked for advice or guidance has helped me in the past. I will go completely out of my way to make sure I am able to reciprocate in some way. I'm an extremely loyal person. So if you've helped me in any way, I will help you out of respect, not obligation. We all need to be grateful for people who make time for us."

Once you have established an initial conversation with a dormant tie, either in person or by phone or video conference, you might want to inject *positive reminiscence* early in the conversation. Positive reminiscence is a psychological term defined as a free-flowing way to remember the good times you have had with someone. Psychologists have shown positive reminiscence techniques improve communication skills, reduce stress, and build connection. Here are some things to think about in using positive reminiscence to reconnect with someone:

- **Remembering Specific Events** – Think about a past event with that person. What was favorable about it? What did it mean to you?
- **Sharing Your Memories** – Then share your memory of that event with the person to let them know you were thinking of them.

Sharing your memories might sound nostalgic, and it is. Social science research actually supports using a nostalgia-based approach in repairing, developing, and strengthening relationships. According to research by Drs. Andrew Abeyta, Clay Routledge, and Jacob Juhl, "Nostalgia increased a sense of confidence in one's social abilities, which in turn motivated more optimism and intentions for resolving a relationship conflict." The authors further observed that "nostalgic reflection inspires people to connect with others." In their research, participants who reflected on a nostalgic memory "reported stronger intentions to pursue goals of connecting with their friends. Nostalgia is not merely relevant to one's social past. It has important implications for one's social future."

Another question my clients often ask is, "Do I need to apologize for not being in touch?" Of course, you don't NEED to apologize. There is no "victim" here. Losing touch is a natural event and getting back in touch should be as well. What you SHOULD be doing is showing appreciation, remembering events, and sharing nostalgic memories with them. Nostalgia is one of your superpowers in getting back in touch, rekindling relationships, and even motivating you to do even MORE reconnecting.

EXAMPLES OF PEOPLE WHO ARE HAPPY TO HELP

A third-generation actor, Spencer Garrett has not forgotten the goodwill people in Hollywood have shown him during his successful acting career. He has made appearances in *Once Upon a Time...In Hollywood, Mad Men, Iron Man 3, Law & Order, Grey's Anatomy, NCIS, JAG, Murder She Wrote,* and *Air Force One.* When I spoke with him, he was filming an HBO LA Lakers project in the role of the famous announcer Chick Hearn. "I feel lucky that I've been doing this a long time," Garett reflects. "And in the last couple of years, it's felt like people have come out of the woodwork, whom I haven't seen in a long time." Garrett gets requests from other actors such as, "You're doing really well, and I'm up for this part. Would you mind putting in a word to the casting director for me?" He observes, "In a lot of cases, it's people you haven't heard from in a long time. And I understand that because I was once that person." Overall, Garrett is happy to provide the favor. Why? "Because I was that person who did that twenty-five years ago," he says. Garret is also a "giver" and thinks about this in a straightforward way: "It all comes back to helping each other out," he says, "I try to do it as much as I can."

For Chris Lu, who shared his philosophy on trust in Chapter 3, the amount of time someone has not been in touch is really not an issue. "There are people who I may not have talked to for ten or fifteen years," he says, "who I will go out of my way to help if they reach out to me. There are also people who I will likely never ever help." For Lu, an individual's integrity is a critical factor in determining whether he will help them. "If you've done something that I think is dishonest in some way, or you're not a person of integrity, I'm not going to help."

AN EXAMPLE OF HOW *NOT* TO GET BACK IN TOUCH

In Chapter 3, Mary K Young shared her thoughts on trust. She also remembers how someone, whom she trusted, did not get back in touch kindly. "I had a friend, who I was very close to at one point," she recalls, "He called me up out of the blue. It had been ten years, and he called to say he was going to be in town." Young was thrilled, "This is someone I was very close to. I brought him out to the house to meet my family. It was like no time had passed, and we had a really nice evening." She mentioned after learning about his work that she wouldn't previously have purchased his services. However, she remembers one big sales ask behind the entire reconnection. "All he really wanted to do was sell me on his firm doing some work for my association," Young said, "And he kept talking about it." Finally, she had to tell him, 'I don't hire outside firms. There's another group in the association that does that. I can introduce you to them.'" She *actually* wanted to help her friend, but he didn't get it. Young laments that "he didn't ever take that bait. Those are situations where the outreach was entirely inappropriate."

There is no "right" way to reconnect. No formula will work every time. However, if your approach includes gratitude, nostalgia, and decreasing time pressure, you increase your chances of success. Also, as we learned from Young's story, the desire to reconnect should be genuine, regardless of how you can help each other. Even if nothing comes of a reconnection right away, you will have rekindled a relationship with someone you genuinely like, which is a benefit in and of itself.

YOUR RELATIONSHIP TO INFINITY TAKEAWAYS

- Reconnect with your network using email or direct message, so the person can respond on their own timeline.
- Positive memories and nostalgia facilitate reconnections with people.
- People are often willing to help, even if you have not been in touch.
- The next chapter will give you tactical advice on leveraging associations in your keep-in-touch strategy.

YOUR REFLECTION QUESTIONS

- Throughout these chapters, you have been making lists of your strong and weak ties and your current and dormant ties. For each person listed, what is one positive memory about them?
- Can you make a plan to share that memory with them?

CHAPTER 8

Associations: In the Room Where It Happens

———

A book about keeping in touch without making a *Hamilton* reference? Surely, you are mistaken. Jefferson, Madison, and Hamilton struck the Great Compromise over dinner in "the room where it happens." This begs the question: Are *you* in the room where it happens for your own career?

I have always disliked the term "networking events." The name misses the keep-in-touch point entirely. Building and keeping an authentic social network is not about any one event. Social media contains endless, cliched career and business development advice articles on where to stand, what to say, or even how to network virtually. Seriously? In Chapter 3, we learned earning trust is a multi-layered process. In Chapter 5, we learned building relationships and friendships can take hundreds of hours. One event won't change your life.

However, investing your valuable time in associations could, in fact, change your career trajectory. In Chapter 6, we learned how Linda's involvement in the Corporate Counsel Women of Color (CCWC) provided her inspiration, support, and structure to keep in touch. Linda's involvement in CCWC and her keep-in-touch activities eventually helped her land a job as a General Counsel.

Getting and staying involved in an association allows for continuous connection and reconnection. Associations provide structure, which can make them the ultimate convener of people who share common interests, professional and personal. Making time for these groups, whether a university alumni association or a professional association of health lawyers, can only help you keep in touch with people who share your interests, background, and experiences. As remote and hybrid work continues, association involvement will be an even more important pillar in your keep-in-touch strategy.

ASSOCIATIONS HELPED ME LAND A JOB IN FRANCE AND INTRODUCED ME TO MY FUTURE WIFE

I am admittedly a bit biased: associations absolutely changed my own life. In 1999, I was a Rotary Ambassadorial Scholar studying international business in Lyon, France. While I was there, I started participating in an association of former French Rotary Scholars in France, known as the ABFR. The group organized weekend events with local Rotary clubs in Paris, Reims/Epernay (champagne country), and Briançon (southern French Alps). These cultural events allowed me to connect not only with Rotarians and their families but also with other Rotary scholars living in different French cities.

Directly following my studies in Lyon, my ABFR relation-ships led me to a job with a French management consulting firm in Paris (now part of KPMG France). I became the first non-French president of the association, and I felt so sup-ported in my new role by the French Rotary community.

As the organizer of the group's cultural events, I found joy in welcoming Rotary Scholars into France from fifteen-plus different countries, using French as a common language. In 2001, at one of the first ABFR events I organized, I met a lovely, red-headed Rotary Scholar from Pennsylvania. That initial meeting sparked a continuing friendship over the coming years. She, too, was good at keeping in touch, with the occasional email and update. In 2004, we were both at Georgetown. She was in law school, and I was starting my MBA. We started dating, and in 2008, we got married.

CASE STUDY: ASSOCIATION INVOLVEMENT FROM THE ORGANIZER PERSPECTIVE

JD Kathuria is the CEO and founder of WashingtonExec, a professional association focused on government contract-ing. WashingtonExec has 475-plus executive members who participate in twenty-five private mission-oriented council groups and hosts over one hundred private events annually in the Washington, DC area. In addition to in-person and virtual events, WashingtonExec publishes a daily newsletter for executives that reaches twenty-thousand-plus subscribers in the DC metro area.

Kathuria is an introvert by nature and admits his work with WashingtonExec encouraged him to behave more like an extrovert. Kathuria founded WashingtonExec because he wanted to create a forum for government contractors to come together. "In government contracting, there's a business need for you to know your competition because there's so much teaming, partnering, and merger and acquisition activity," he said. "It's not like other industries where the need to meet your competition is lower. I equate it to an opportunity to be fierce competitors during the day and friendly competitive mates overnight."

By participating in WashingtonExec's community, members are often surprised by what they learn about what is going on in the industry and what the executives are going through. Kathuria observed, "Executives share information with people they like, know, and trust. There is a business intelligence aspect to the relationship. There is a personal aspect to the relationship. People talk about their dogs, their vacations, and their kids going to high school or college." Kathuria has seen firsthand the benefits that accrue to government contracting executives who take leadership roles within the organization. "If you're the chairperson of an event," he observed, "people remember that more than just someone who's a regular participant." Kathuria equates participating in WashingtonExec with going to the gym. He said, "You can join all the best gyms in the world, but if you don't go, it won't help you that much."

ASSOCIATION INVOLVEMENT HELPED ADVANCE AN EXECUTIVE'S CAREER

Sadhvi Subramanian, the former Senior Vice President at Capital One whom we met in Chapter 7, has become a champion for active participation in professional associations. She credits her time at Chevy Chase Bank for getting her outside of her comfort zone. Originally from Delhi, India, she knew she needed to get acclimated to the American business culture. "I really did not know how to sell my talent for myself in the US," she said. "It was a skill that I had to learn, and my direct supervisors really encouraged me to join industry organizations." Subramanian believes most people should join associations "because you build your own personal network. And then, by having your own personal network, you are able to bring back information to the organization that others may not have."

She believes deeply by investing time in association relationships, "you end up learning so much more than reading articles online or on the phone. You can learn about trends in the industry, who is acquiring what, who's going to be looking for a loan, and who is partnering with whom."

Her approach to industry associations has also evolved as she has participated in them. "When I started getting involved," she said, "I was just a member and would go for the events. Now, I would do it a little bit differently. I would get involved upfront, join committees, and try to get to the executive level within the industry organization."

She also encourages her direct reports to do the same. "I encourage everybody in our group and on our team to join industry organizations." With some of her direct reports, she observes that "there is resistance initially because you're taking away from my time, and I'm going to have to work an hour longer if I go for this lunch or event. Once they've done it for a couple of years, however, they realize the value and really appreciate it."

Subramanian admits in the beginning, her industry organization participation was not strategic but rather more organic. "It just happened, and I seized the moment." She remembers, for example, sitting at Northern Virginia Commercial Real Estate Women (CREW) lunch. "I was a member of the North Virginia CREW, but a member of DC CREW said, 'hey, do you want to join my committee?' Somehow it worked out that I was able to transfer my membership to the DC chapter. I became active in that committee, and that's when I realized I really enjoyed this! This is what being part of an organization means."

Subramanian later moved up into the higher ranks of CREW. "I was able to get on the board, and then I had a couple of people approach me and ask, 'why don't you go for president?'" Ultimately, she accepted and was glad she did. "As president, I put together an advisory board with very senior women," she said. "We used to meet often during 2012, and I received a lot of valuable advice from these women who agreed to do this just because they wanted to help. Now, we're good friends. We all get together every second or third month, just to have lunch." As a result, Subramanian has built a network of trusted relationships because of her multiyear commitment to CREW.

DOING GOOD WHILE CONVENING PEOPLE WITHIN YOUR AUTHENTIC PROFESSIONAL NETWORK

Subramanian also likes to keep in touch with people via philanthropic events. "Working at a bank," she recalls, "you have tables at charity events. So I make sure I invite longstanding clients and partners." She once said yes to having Capital One contribute to a charity event for one of her clients. But then she asked herself, "how am I going to fill this table in New York?" "I called up a few clients and partners, and everybody said, 'Sure, I'll come.' We all went up to New York and had a great time. We've now attended that same event together for seven years."

Subramanian wants to continue improving the cohesion of this group of senior women. She does this by trying to "get a couple of new people every year. It's probably a group of about twenty to twenty-five people now." Subramanian loves the synergy between the women who come, and she learns a lot from all of them every time they get together." "This has organically turned into the best networking event," she believes, "as it is very intimate."

When it comes to networks, Subramanian believes that "different things work for different people. You have to try everything and then figure out where you're comfortable. It takes time. For example, it may take thirty events before you figure out what works for you. You really have to push yourself to show up because that's the first thing, right? Once you show up, then you will make the effort."

"If you don't make the effort to show up," Subramanian explains, "you're not going to be able to network. And the more you do it, the more comfortable you get with it. Joining an industry organization is great because you build your network organically and network with business associates who are all working toward a common goal for the organization.

By joining a programs committee meeting every month, you're actually working with people in an informal setting, and you are getting to know them much better than just meeting them at a cocktail."

YOUR RELATIONSHIP TO INFINITY TAKEAWAYS

- Associations are a great investment of your time and are an excellent way to keep in touch with others in your profession or industry.
- You can develop both professional and personal relationships within an association.
- Attending one event usually does not lead to significant outcomes. Association involvement takes repeated annual commitment.
- Taking a leadership role in an association is a great way to raise your profile and meet people.
- Introverts and extroverts alike can succeed in association leadership roles.
- The next chapter will provide tactics on using LinkedIn to improve your approach to keeping in touch.

YOUR REFLECTION QUESTIONS

- Are you a member of a professional association? If not, which one might you explore?
- Are you a member of an alumni association? If not, which one might you join?
- How might you take a leadership role in one of the professional or alumni organizations that interest you?

CHAPTER 9

Using LinkedIn to Advance Your Keeping-in-Touch Priorities

———

I wanted the LinkedIn chapter of this book to be toward the end, to establish solid relationship principles before discussing specific tools. LinkedIn is like your keep-in-touch minivan because it's big, can fit many people, and goes long distances. However, you need to map out your destination and enter the right GPS coordinates first. This entire book has been about connection and reconnection in personal and professional life. LinkedIn can be incredibly helpful to you in keeping in touch with both dormant ties and current ties, as well as strong ties and weak ties. Having spent time developing focused strategies that prioritize your relationships, you are now in a place to leverage LinkedIn to advance your keeping in touch goals.

BENEFITS OF LINKEDIN 101

LinkedIn was founded in Reid Hoffman's living room in 2002 and officially launched on May 5, 2003. At the recommendation of a friend, I joined LinkedIn in January 2004 while living in Paris. When I joined LinkedIn, I received a member number, which was 141,272. As of 2021, LinkedIn now has 774M+ users in two-hundred-plus countries. As an early adopter of LinkedIn, I have leveraged the platform for over seventeen years to stay in touch with friends, classmates, colleagues, supervisors, clients, and business partners. LinkedIn allows you to build relationships online and support your professional efforts in seeking a new job or potentially building a professional services practice.

USING LINKEDIN IN CONJUNCTION WITH EXCEL

In Chapter 2, Everett Hutt showed us how he prioritizes his relationships. He agrees LinkedIn is useful for keeping in touch, but it is not his only tool. Before joining LinkedIn, Hutt started an Excel file to help remind him about people in his network. In Chapter 7, we learned about the importance of remembering and sharing positive things about people. Hutt embeds this type of reminder in his Excel file. "I indicate the year I met them and in what context." His Excel file helps him keep track of his relationships, while technology is used for outreach. "Depending on the relationship, I will use LinkedIn direct message or email," Hutt says.

Hutt does his best to keep track of the career changes of people in his network. "If I do see a change on LinkedIn, I'll congratulate them," he says, "If it's a personal friend, I'll send a Christmas or holiday card once a year. I also like to write personal notes of congratulations. If I see a useful article, I'll forward it to them."

AN AUTHENTIC APPROACH TO LINKEDIN FOCUSING ON QUALITY OF RELATIONSHIPS

Hutt has also personally seen the negative side and overwhelm that can come with social media. "After joining Salesforce," he said, "I received LinkedIn connections from hundreds of people I didn't know, which I turned down." I agree with Hutt's approach to LinkedIn. His criterion for accepting a LinkedIn connection request is "Can I actually remember them, working with them and interacting with them? It has to be somebody I want to stay in touch with." Hutt elaborates, "I'm not interested in the quantity."

ACTIONABLE LINKEDIN TIPS

Here are some actionable tips for using LinkedIn to maintain your relationships

1. **Connect with current/weak, current/strong, dormant/ weak, and dormant/strong ties** – I agree with Hutt that you should connect on LinkedIn only with people you know. You should, however, be sure to connect with as many of your ties as possible. A great question to ask yourself is, "Do my LinkedIn connections reflect all my ties?" One strategy I use with my clients to help them remember their connections is to review their resume. I ask, "Who did you work with?" and "Did you have a positive experience with them?" If the answer is yes and

yes, then make sure you are connected to them on LinkedIn. Each person who connects with you on LinkedIn becomes a first-degree connection. Any person who has connected with them on LinkedIn becomes a second-degree connection.

2. **Your LinkedIn profile should include accurate dates for when you attended university and worked in prior roles** – By putting accurate dates and information in your LinkedIn profile regarding your education and employment, you can more easily identify your current and weak ties from those time periods.

3. **Email works just as well as LinkedIn direct messenger** – When you connect with someone on LinkedIn, you can often see their email address by clicking on "contact info." Writing them an email is just as simple as sending them a direct message. Some people also do not check LinkedIn very often, so an email may reach them faster.

4. **Celebrate wins** – Your connections are talking about their promotions, new jobs, new clients, and new degrees/ certifications on LinkedIn. It is a good use of time to acknowledge their achievement with a quick "like" and short, direct message of congratulations.

5. **Use targeted searches to uncover dormant and weak ties** – In all honesty, LinkedIn is one big search party. When you reconnect with past clients, friends, classmates, colleagues, partners, and vendors, you increase your broader network on LinkedIn. This allows you to perform targeted searches when evaluating potential roles for new

employment in an organization or selling services for your professional services practice.

a. **Maximize "My Network"** – By clicking on "My Network" and then clicking "Connections," you can search all of your first-degree connections with search filters. Some of my favorite searches and queries to run are:

- *Searches by Location* – Let's say you are about to take a trip to Washington, DC. You can run a filter search on your current first-degree LinkedIn connections to see who is currently living in Washington, DC. If you have time, you can reach out to specific people to get back in touch while you are in town.

- *Searches by Company* – You can identify people working at specific companies of interest. Search the people in your current LinkedIn network (both first- and second-degree connections) by searching on specific employers. Let's say you are interested in Amazon. You can search your current LinkedIn connections to see if either current or former employees in your relationship base work at Amazon.

- *Role Searches* – Let's say you want to identify chief marketing officers or vice presidents of finance or general counsel who are first- or second-degree connections. You can search "My Network" by typing in the "Title'" within the search box. By doing these searches periodically, you can even identify your first-degree connections who have received promotions or moved to new organizations. This becomes another opportunity to offer a note of congratulations and keep in touch.

b. **Alumni Searches** – In addition to the "My Network" feature, you can also search the alumni page of your undergraduate and graduate school. Type the institution you graduated from into the LinkedIn search box. Each university has its own LinkedIn page. An alumni tab within the university page allows you to perform targeted searches. (You can locate the "alumni" tab between the "jobs" tab and the "insights" tab.) For example, let's say you want to identify classmates in your same graduation year. You can run a date of graduation search on the alumni page by inputting the beginning and ending dates of your enrollment. You can also identify alumni who live in your city and filter them by their employer.

c. **Employer Searches** – Most companies have their own LinkedIn page. You can go directly to the company's page to identify current employees and your first-degree connections who work there.

CASE EXAMPLE – LINKEDIN SUPPORTING A RETIREMENT TRANSITION

In chapter 4, I shared the story of a retiring law firm partner named Mark. As Mark was retiring from his firm, I remember him saying, "I am on LinkedIn, but frankly, I have no idea what to do with it." The more Mark and I talked about his past colleagues, clients, peer board members, and classmates, he began to realize how many people he had lost touch with.

We began a manageable goal of five reconnections per week on LinkedIn, which eventually led to some actual live conversations. Many of his dormant strong ties and dormant weak ties were so glad to reconnect with Mark. Mark was amazed at how easy it was to search and sort based on his undergraduate and law school classes to see what his classmates were doing. One of the people he reconnected with through LinkedIn identified a nonprofit that aligned with his values and suggested he reach out. At his friend's suggestion, he approached the organization. He was eventually hired by this social mission nonprofit, where he served on their leadership team for eight years. With a clear goal in mind, Mark used LinkedIn to support his retirement transition.

YOUR RELATIONSHIP TO INFINITY TAKEAWAYS

- LinkedIn is an excellent way to keep in touch with strong, weak, dormant, and current ties.
- An Excel file can be a useful tool to complement your LinkedIn connections by setting up specific reminders and inputting contact information.
- Ensure your LinkedIn profile is complete and contains accurate information. This will help you connect with past classmates and colleagues.
- Quick notes of congratulations are a great way to keep in touch with your network using LinkedIn. A personal, handwritten note is also a nice touch.
- The next chapter will showcase executives' perspectives on how keeping in touch has helped their careers.

YOUR REFLECTION QUESTIONS

- Is your LinkedIn profile complete?
- Have you connected with your past classmates and colleagues?
- How often are you celebrating other people's wins on LinkedIn?
- Have you set up an Excel file to help remind yourself of the people in your network?

CHAPTER 10

Executives' Perspectives: Keep in Touch and Reap the Benefits

———

In his time at FiscalNote, CEO Tim Hwang has raised more than $230M in venture capital and acquisition financing from *The Economist*, S&P Global, Mark Cuban, Jerry Yang, Steve Case, and NEA. Hwang has been profiled in *Forbes* 30 Under 30, *Washingtonian*'s Tech Titans, *Inc.* 30 Under 30, Goldman Sachs 2020 Builders and Innovators, *CNN*'s Top 10 Startups, and *Business Insider*'s Top 25 Hottest Startups. He is, in my opinion, the perfect example of someone who reaps all the benefits of keeping in touch.

Hwang is the son of Korean immigrants who moved to the DC metro area and worked for the federal government. Growing up near the nation's capital, he became very interested in both politics and technology. As he began to get in involved in politics, Hwang realized the value of relationships. "I internalized this idea from a really early age that your network is your net worth. All of the outcomes of your life can be determined, almost purely based on the deep relationships with people you know. That inflow of information comes purely from having good relationships with people. These relationships can be built on something as simple as meeting up with somebody for dinner on a Friday and just getting some tidbits on certain things."

Hwang believes networking is "about the exchange of value and not a transaction. I view my career as a decade's long endeavor, but it is important to find people who have similar values and interests. Even if the thing that I'm working on right now does not intersect with one of my contacts at the moment, in the back of my mind, I'm thinking maybe we will work on something together in the future. Life and work weave in and out. I think I focus a lot on that."

The research supports Tim's point of view. According to *Network Drivers of Success*, "Decades of research on organizational networks have shown that who you know—and who knows you—is critical to performance and career success. People in positive relationships are more likely to share valuable information, such as available job opportunities and insights into organizational politics, recommend each other for opportunities, vouch for each other, and provide work-related advice and support."

In my coaching practice, I have seen the transformation firsthand when my executive clients decide to prioritize keeping in touch. In the process, they uncover and rediscover:

FIVE CAREER BENEFITS OF KEEPING IN TOUCH

1. Mentor and sponsor relationships
2. Friendships
3. Ideas, insights, and relevant introductions for career and retirement transitions
4. Job promotions and advancement opportunities
5. Business development insights for their professional services practices

In the rest of this chapter, successful executives in the private and public sectors share their unique perspectives on how keeping in touch has made a significant difference in their career trajectories.

1. MENTOR AND SPONSOR RELATIONSHIPS

In "Understanding the Impact of Mentorship Versus Sponsorship," *Forbes*, Katharine Mobley asserts that "both mentorship and sponsorship create and reinforce connections within the workforce." "Sponsors act as spotlights," she says, who are internal to the organization. Mobley defines the goal of sponsorship as "Promotion," where "sponsors actively endorse their sponsored party and work to elevate that person's status within an organization."

In contrast to a sponsor's role of promotion, a mentor serves to "offer advice and guidance along the way," says Mosely. "And unlike sponsorship, mentor-mentee relationships can be a two-way street, wherein sometimes the roles reverse. It's also possible to have multiple mentors at one time. These relationships don't always last forever, which is why mentors can also be external to your organization."

Keeping in touch can help you build mentor and sponsor relationships in multiple ways. Divina Gamble is the DC Office Managing Partner at Korn Ferry, the largest executive search and talent solutions firm in the world, believes keep-in-touch efforts should focus on both mentorship and sponsorship. Gamble is a Senior Client Partner, Nonprofit Philanthropy and Social Enterprise practice co-leader, and a member of the firm's Board & CEO and Diversity practices. Regarding relationship building in your organization, she says, "It's not just about finding somebody who will be a mentor, but you must understand the importance of sponsorship." Particularly in a larger firm, she advises, it is important "to build many different relationships because often you need multiple sponsors to help you progress." She encourages people to get outside of their comfort zones. She says, "Don't limit yourself to just working with one or two people but find ways you can be more well-known in other circles across your company."

Complementing Gamble's perspective on sponsorship, Mary K Young provides insights into the value of peer-to-peer executive mentor relationships. Young is a Partner at Zeughauser Group, where she advises senior law firm leaders on growth, market trends, and positioning. She believes in the power of peer-to-peer mentoring relationships. "At Zeughauser," she said, "we recognize that specifically for executives, such as law firm chairs and CEOs, there is a tremendous amount of value in forming relationships with people in similar roles." Young continues, "Within a law firm, there is only one Chief Marketing Officer (CMO) and one chair. These are the types of leaders who are in a situation where no one else in the law firm can really understand their work." Young advocates for participation in executive-level roundtables which allow for peer-to-peer information sharing.

2. FRIENDSHIPS

Chapter 5 explored the social science behind friendships. Young says she has kept in touch to foster not only mentor relationships but friendships as well. She admits this did not come naturally to her when she was in her twenties, but ultimately, investing in work relationships has enriched her life. "I would say the best friends I have in my life are people that I've met at work. For example, I have a friend from my days in the [Jimmy Carter] White House, and we're close. While I never thought of keeping in touch with these friends as advancing my career, doing so has been helpful." Young reflects on her dormant and current friendships, noting that "some blossom into real, significant friendships. Other relationships I see people occasionally." Young's approach is authentic. "If the conversation eventually leads to winning new work, then great. If it never does, then that's fine too."

3. CAREER AND RETIREMENT TRANSITIONS

Jeremy Butler, Navy veteran who shared his thoughts on trust in Chapter 3, provides a unique perspective on how keeping in touch can help us through career and retirement changes. He is a big believer in the power of relationships to support us during significant life transitions. His experience comes from both his service in the Navy and his transition to a national nonprofit.

Butler credits his successful career transition from military service to his current organization to an introduction from his wife. "There is an organization called Joining Forces, created under President Barack Obama, First Lady Michelle Obama, and then Second Lady Jill Biden. This organization works with military and veteran organizations. My wife worked for the First Lady, whose office was responsible for running the program. My wife introduced me to the Army Colonel running the program. He was willing to sit down with me and give me his thoughts on veteran organizations. He said I really should reach out to IAVA, and he put me in touch with them."

"It was relationships," Jeremy emphasizes, that certainly got me in the door. At the time, IAVA was not hiring. Following the introduction, I started to talk to people at IAVA and stayed in touch. IAVA created a role for me, which ultimately led to my being hired."

4. JOB PROMOTIONS

Keeping in touch and nurturing relationships is critical to upward career movement within organizations, too. While in the Navy, Butler found that "relationships and trust are especially important at the officer level and at the senior enlisted level." In the Navy, he says, "it's a board that determines your professional future. And by 'boards,' I mean a group of your peers. The board looks at your record and makes a determination based on the facts, as well as what they have heard as to your qualifications for next commands."

Navy officers are ranked everywhere from zero to one hundred percent in their "confidence factor." "Humans are there making these decisions," Butler explains. "They may be told to focus primarily on the facts. However, I believe your reputation as an officer also carries a lot of weight." Butler advises officers to focus on relationships. He says, "I tell officers and others that it's not just about what you've done, it's how you've done it."

"Relationships and keeping in touch matters," says Butler. "People are probably going to remember less about the assignments you had and more about the type of leader you've been, the type of relationships you've forged, and the type of person you were."

5. NEW CLIENTS AND DEVELOPING A PROFESSIONAL SERVICE PRACTICE

Keeping in touch also has an important role in building a professional services practice. Divina Gamble's philosophy in building her executive search practice at Korn Ferry was founded in "doing good work, building trusted relationships, and giving honest counsel." "After we're done with an engagement, I try to stay in touch with both the placement and the client to see how things are going," she says. Gamble makes the time to focus on these relationships. She said, "It's about spending time. Going to breakfast or lunch with both the candidates and with the placements. It's also important to stay in touch with the people who don't get the job." This authentic approach has helped her succeed in her practice. "Some of my first business actually came in as a result of taking the time to have conversations with job seekers," she reflects. Gamble does not consider herself a big networker or schmoozer. Rather, she believes her success came from "just treating people well, which ended up turning into business later. Staying in touch is part of treating people well."

When Mary K Young became a Partner at Zeughauser, she also needed to be able to bring in her own clients. Building and maintaining relationships helped her frame from servicing internal clients to building a book of business. Admittedly, she felt "initially awkward about sales. I wanted to continue the close relationships I had as a CMO of a law firm," Young reflects, "I formed a lot of friendships in the CMO community, and I didn't want people to think that I was trying to sell to them." She admits, "I had to navigate that with existing relationships. I was a little bit worried that I would appear inappropriate or not authentic. It took me a few years to get away from that." What helped Young the most was focusing on listening to her clients' needs. As she likes to advise anyone developing business, the client wants you to "tell me about my lawn, not about your grass seed."

YOUR RELATIONSHIP TO INFINITY TAKEAWAYS
- Keeping in touch reaps amazing benefits.
- As an executive, having peer-to-peer relationships is important to navigating your career. Professional roundtables can help you develop and maintain these relationships.
- The next chapter will help you take everything you learned in *Relationships to Infinity* so you can kick off your keep-in-touch journey.

YOUR REFLECTION QUESTIONS
- How might keeping in touch benefit your career?
- Of the five benefits outlined in this chapter, which one(s) apply to you?

CHAPTER 11

Strategies for Keeping in Touch

Congratulations! You are now keep-in-touch "certified." You have all the tools you need. The next step is to bring *Relationships to Infinity: The Art and Science of Keeping in Touch* to life.

Keeping in touch is about YOU. You decide how much time you want to invest. You decide whom to reach out to. You decide the pace of keeping in touch with your authentic social network.

This book has not been about getting you to reach out to every person you have ever met. Throughout your career, it is completely normal for acquaintances and friendships to come and go. For example, you may now have less in common with people you were once close to ten, fifteen, or twenty years ago. Relationships do not need to last forever. Rekindling dormant ties can, however, add a great deal of meaning and satisfaction to your life.

CONFIDENCE IN KEEPING IN TOUCH

Embarking on strategies to keep in touch needs requires confidence. And by confidence, I mean more than just pumping you up with false hope. Harvard Business School Professor Dr. Rosebeth Moss Kanter, author of *Confidence: How Winning Streaks and Losing Streaks Begin and End,* defines confidence as "an expectation of a positive outcome. It is not a personality trait; it is an assessment of a situation that sparks motivation. If you have confidence, you're motivated to put in the effort, to invest the time and resources, and to persist in reaching the goal. It's not confidence itself that produces success; it's the investment and the effort. Without enough confidence, it's too easy to give up prematurely or not get started at all. Hopelessness and despair prevent positive action."

To get started, you need not believe every person you reach out to will respond favorably or that every relationship you rekindle will bear amazing fruit. "Confidence involves a dose of reality," Kanter explains. "It is not blind optimism, thinking that everything will be fine no matter what. Confidence stems from knowing that there will be mistakes, problems, and small losses *en route* to big wins. After all, even winning sports teams are often behind at some point in the game. Confidence grows when you look at what can go wrong, think through alternatives, and feel you are prepared for whatever might happen."

This book is full of individuals who experimented with keeping in touch and grew their confidence in the process. In Chapter 1, for example, we learned about Usha Chaudhary's underlying confidence, as she bounced back from both personal tragedy and career adversity to develop an authentic social network. In Chapter 4, we saw Kevin DeSanto's confidence, as he pushed himself to build a successful investment banking business despite being a natural introvert. In Chapter 6, Linda showed confidence in her career transition when she worked through her Bermuda Keep-in-Touch Triangle to land her General Counsel role.

Here are some strategies to make *Relationships to Infinity* come to life for you.

TELL OTHERS ABOUT YOUR KEEP-IN-TOUCH INTENTIONS

The best way to succeed in building a keep-in-touch habit is to share your intentions with others. Don't keep your keep-in-touch goals a secret. Shout them from the rooftops!

Take heed of this interesting research by Professor Gail Matthews, "Strategies for achieving goals, resolutions" who uncovered some key secrets to achieving your goals. Her study showed you are:

- 43 percent more likely to achieve your plan if you write it down
- 62 percent more likely to achieve your plan if you write it down *and* share it with a friend
- 76 percent more likely to achieve your plan if you write it down, share it with a friend, and send weekly progress to a friend

To make your keep-in-touch habit real, be sure you include someone else in the plan to hold you accountable.

MAKE YOUR EXCEL FILE LIST! – REVIEW YOUR STRONG, WEAK, CURRENT AND DORMANT TIES

Do not overthink this. As you have gone through this book, I am sure you have thought of people with whom you'd like to get back in touch. If you are struggling to think of a few, ask yourself these questions:

- Who has supported you during your career or at a particular moment in time?
- Who energizes you when you meet with them?

Go ahead. Open an Excel file. Create the following fields 1) First Name, 2) Last Name, 3) Postal Address, 4) Email Address, 5) Cell Phone, 6) Last Date Contacted, 7) How You Know Them, and 8) Favorite Memory.

The Chapter 2 reflection questions asked you to outline your strong ties and weak ties, as well as your current and dormant ties. To start populating this Excel file, you can turn to these lists and enter the names of these individuals.

A simple action you can take within your file is to note a significant annual date to reach out to the person. Some people like to mark birthdays and anniversaries. In business, people sometimes like to mark the beginning of a new client relationship or the moment a big contract landed. Every year, I hear from my real estate agent, Eva Davis, on the date we closed on our house. Her outreach always serves as a great reminder of the work she put in, so we could be in our current home.

MAKE THE TIME – LITERALLY: TIME BLOCKING AND GOAL SETTING

Just as Linda in Chapter 6 made her "Connection Calls" a scheduled and regular part of her week, you, too, can use time blocking to get into a keep-in-touch habit. Keeping in touch can easily become part of your week or your month. A common complaint from my clients about keeping in touch is that "I don't have time." It is not as if you need to block an entire day to keep in touch. What if you spent fifteen minutes a week getting in touch with one person you know, like, and trust? At the end of the year, you will have connected or reconnected with fifty-two people.

Your action is to find the best time in your calendar. If you are a night owl, draft an email at night and then send it (or schedule it to auto-send) the following morning. If you are a morning person, do your keep-in-touch activities as part of your morning routine.

MINDSET SHIFT: JUST START

In Chapter 6, you learned about the Bermuda Keep-In-Touch triangle and how to not fall into the trap of self-sabotage. Executives often complain they "are not good at keeping in touch." Why? The idea of reconnecting seems daunting because of all the people you think you would need to reconnect with. Instead of lumping everyone together, identify one person. Who would be the first person you would want to get back in touch with? Getting started can be as easy as sending an email to someone saying, "I know I have been out of touch and wanted to see how you are doing."

POSITIVE MEMORIES FOUNDED IN APPRECIATION AND GRATITUDE

Chapter 7 taught us that keeping in touch is also about appreciation and sharing positive memories. No doubt you did many wonderful things throughout your career. Imagine if you began your day with a mental stroll through your career, reflecting on everything you learned. Who helped you get there? What did they do for you? What was unique about their kindness or generosity?

To bring Chapter 7 to life, your action is simple. Let a single person know you are thinking about them and want to catch up. You can use a letter, a text, an email, or a phone call. Whatever you feel most comfortable doing. Let them know you are thinking of them and what you appreciate about them.

JOIN AND GET ACTIVE IN AN ASSOCIATION

In Chapter 8, we learned about all the benefits of associations. Sadhvi Subramanian got active in CREW and found fulfillment from being in a leadership role. She found it so useful she encouraged her direct reports to get involved in associations. What are you waiting for?

CELEBRATE SUCCESS

Celebrating success is yet another wonderful opportunity to reach out and reconnect. A friend gets a promotion. A former colleague lands a new job. A former classmate lands a new client. It's time to celebrate! You will likely learn about this news either from colleagues in the industry or through an update on the person's LinkedIn profile. You can now send a quick email or note of congratulations. This is an event you can also mark in your Excel file.

Want to up your celebration? Have on hand a batch of congratulations cards. Sending a real letter or card still has an impact and tends to be extremely well-received.

GO KEEP IN TOUCH!

The strategies outlined above are for YOU! They begin with you because they center on the relationships you already have. Send out a congratulations note. Offer a thank you to someone who has been helpful in your career. Just start, and send me a note through my website, www.readysetlaunch.net, to let me know how it goes!

Acknowledgments

———

This book would not have been possible without my talented wife and best friend, Lori Mihalich-Levin. You have read every word of this book (often multiple times) and have shown extreme patience as it evolved. An author in your own right, I have valued both your thoughts on my approach to structuring my stories and your editorial eye. You never gave up on this project. You never gave up on me. I love you. Thank you for all you do.

I am forever grateful to my caring parents, Lawrence and Phyllis Levin. Your undying support and love throughout my life have given me an incredible foundation. Always believing in my potential, you encouraged my curiosity and independent streak early on. The platform you provided allowed me to take risks and become who I am today. I have learned many life lessons from both of you. Thank you both for supporting this book.

My grandparents, Gertrude and Bernard Klapman, gave me a real-world example of what it was like to keep in touch. For twenty years, starting when I graduated from college, I had a phone call every Sunday night with Grandma Gertie (knowing Grandpa Bernie was sitting right next to her). Keeping in touch with them on Sunday nights marked my week. Whether we discussed the price of melons at the grocery store or what I was working on, you always showed genuine curiosity and love. Between our phone calls, you sent me cards and articles in the mail. Keeping in touch was in your DNA and may you both rest in peace.

I appreciate my mother-in-law, Barbara Marlowe, and my father-in-law, Jim Hartye. Thank you both for supporting this book. Your encouragement and editorial comments helped me develop better arguments and narratives. The final product is better because of your loving input.

Those I interviewed for this book injected real-world stories and anecdotes to *Relationships to Infinity.* Your stories and insights helped create the foundation for this book, and your time and support have meant the world to me. In alphabetical order, a big thank you to:

Stacy Blake-Beard, Jeremy Butler, Usha Chaudhary, Kevin DeSanto, Phil de Picciotto, Ann Ford, Divina Gamble, Spencer Garrett, Sherri Harris, Everett Hutt, Tim Hwang, JD Kathuria, Chris Liu, Julissa Marenco, Barbara McDuffie, Brian Peters, Sadhvi Subramanian, and Mary K Young.

While I did not share your incredible stories in *Relationships to Infinity,* I appreciate Cynthia Warrick and Susan Chodakewitz for taking the time to be interviewed on background.

Dean Paul Almeida, at the Georgetown University McDonough School of Business, encouraged me on my project and kindly introduced me to Associate Dean Michael Boyer O'Leary. I enjoyed Dean O'Leary's willingness to share his thoughts on network theory, as well as publications to support the arguments in my book. Dean O'Leary also reviewed some of my chapters and provided insightful feedback.

My friends Mary Louise Stott and Red Gobuty gave me excellent feedback on numerous chapters, and I appreciate your suggestions.

My friend, Stephen Sheehy, has been a wonderful source of encouragement and banter during this book-writing journey. You reviewed parts of this book and delivered insightful comments and feedback.

My friends Julian Ha, Kecia Hansard, and Brendan McElroy provided valuable introductions. I appreciated your encouragement as I shared chapters of the book with you.

My friend, Susan Dunlap, was a great sounding board as we discussed potential chapter ideas.

Andrea Bonoir and Keith Saylor are both talented psychologists. I learned a great deal from our conversations on background. I am grateful our discussions gave me a deeper understanding of human emotions.

Alisa Parenti gave me the incredible idea to write this book with Eric Koester and the Creators Institute. I am so lucky to have worked alongside a cohort of authors pursuing their creative dreams. My developmental editor, Judy Rosen, gave me the structure and accountability to begin writing my early ideas on paper. My editor at New Degree Press, Kathy Wood, provided the right mix of humor and structure to take this manuscript across the finish line. My author coach, John Saunders, gave an endless number of ideas on marketing this book.

My sincerest thanks to the following individuals who provided financial support to produce, *Relationships to Infinity: The Art and Science of Keeping in Touch.* You supported me when the book was just an idea. I am so lucky to have all of you in my corner. In alphabetical order, I am grateful to:

Anat Allal, Danny Allen, Jacques Arsenault, Troy Beeler, Danielle Berman, Subroto Bose, Andrea Bouwman, George Brelsford, Michael Chiswick-Patterson, Mick Cox, Eva Davis, Jessica and Mark Flugge, Jose Garcia, Precious Gittens, Red Gobuty, Cesar Gonzales, Victor Gootee, Jill and Bob Granik, Jen Grunewald, Phillip Hampton, Pamela Hardy, James Hartye and Barbara Marlow, Steve Heller, Michelle Hipwood, Patricia and Matthew Huggins, Chris Jones, William Jones, AT Johnston, Gay Klapman, Eric Koester, Lawrence and Phyllis Levin, Robert E Lewandowski, Joseph E Lynch, Patrick McAuley, Brendan McElroy, Mark Miano, Holly Micozzi, Mary Theresa Migliorelli, Jonathan Milde, Benjamin Nussdorf, Thomas Ortenzi, Elizabeth Owens, Paolo Palma and Shelley Yeh-Palma, Kinari Patel, Kendra Perkins Norwood, Lee Pinkowitz, David Reina, Mandy Schermer MacVey, Susanne Seitinger, Tom Shea, Stephen Sheehy, Tom Spiggle, Michael Spratt, Michael Shattuck, Micah and Nicole Smith, Ari Strait, Eliza and Scott Strickland, Julia and Jordan

Tama, Frederick E Thrasher, Richard Tinimbang, Marilyn Tucker, Arthur Uratani, John Ustica, John Van Name, James Veltri, Jen Wagener, John Walsh, Bill and Mary Wheatley, Eric S Williams, Dale Wright, and Eric Young.

Appendix

───

INTRODUCTION

Grant, Adam. *Give and Take: Why Helping Others Drives Our Success.* New York: Penguin Books, 2014.

LinkedIn. "Eighty-percent of Professionals Consider Networking Important to Career Success." June 22, 2017. https://news.linkedin.com/2017/6/eighty-percent-of-professionals-consider-networking-important-to-career-success.

TED. "Robin Joy Myers: The Science of Loneliness and Isolation." July 29, 2019. Video, 7:17. https://www.youtube.com/watch?v=9qFKPwF8Sac.

Winch, Guy. "10 Surprising Facts About Loneliness." *Psychology Today*, October 21, 2014. https://www.psychologytoday.com/us/blog/the-squeaky-wheel/201410/10-surprising-facts-about-loneliness.

CHAPTER 1

Grant, Adam. *Give and Take: Why Helping Others Drives Our Success.* New York: Penguin Books, 2014.

Surgent CPA Review. "How Hard is the CPA Exam?" Last modified October 17, 2021. https://www.surgentcpareview.com/cpa-exam-resources/how-hard-is-the-cpa-exam/.

CHAPTER 2

Gino, Francesca, Tiziana Casciaro, and Maryam Kouchaki. "Why Connect? Moral Consequences of Networking with a Promotion or Prevention Focus." *American Psychological Association, Journal of Personality and Social Psychology: Attitudes and Social Cognition,* Vol. 119, No. 6 (2020): 1221-38. https://doi.apa.org/doiLanding?doi=10.1037%2Fpspa0000226.

Granovetter, Mark S. "The Strength of Weak Ties." *American Journal of Sociology.* The University of Chicago Press. Vol 78, No.6, (May 1973): 1360-80. http://www.jstor.org/stable/2776392.

Levin, Daniel, Jorge Walter, and Keith Murninghan. "Dormant Ties: The Value of Reconnecting." *Organization Science.* Vol. 22, No. 4 (July-August 2011): 923-39. https://doi.org/10.1287/orsc.1100.0576.

White, Harold. *Chains of Opportunity: System Models of Mobility in Organizations.* Cambridge: Harvard University Press, 1970.

CHAPTER 3

Carboni, Inga, Rob Cross, Aaron Page, and Andrew Parker. "Network Drivers of Success: How Successful Women Manage Their Networks." *Connected Commons,* September 2019.

CHAPTER 4

Bishop Smith, Edward, Tanya Menon, and Leigh Thompson. "Status Differences in the Cognitive Activation of Social Networks." *Organization Science.* Vol 23, No 1 (January-February 2012): 67-82. https://doi.org/10.1287/orsc.1100.0643.

CHAPTER 5

Cook, Gareth. "Why We Are Wired to Connect." *Scientific American,* October 22, 2013. https://www.scientificamerican.com/article/why-we-are-wired-to-connect/.

Degges-White, Suzanne. "The Most Important Element of Any Friendship." *Psychology Today,* August 9, 2016. https://www.psychologytoday.com/us/blog/lifetime-connections/201608/the-most-important-element-any-friendship.

Hall, Jeffrey. "How Many Hours Does It Take to Make a Friend?" *Journal of Social and Personal Relationships,* March 15, 2018.

CHAPTER 7

Abeyta, Andrew A., Clay Routledge, and Jacob Juhl. "Looking Back to Move Forward: Nostalgia as A Psychological Resource for Promoting Relationship Goals and Overcoming Relationship Challenges." *Journal of Personality and Social Psychol-*

ogy, Vol. 109, No. 6 (2015): 1029–1044. https://doi.org/10.1037/
pspi0000036.

Goldfarb, Ann. "Should You Reach Out to a Former Friend Right
Now?" *New York Times,* July 13, 2020. https://www.nytimes.
com/2020/06/02/smarter-living/should-you-reach-out-to-a-
former-friend-right-now.html.

Grant, Adam and Francesca Gino. "A Little Thanks Goes a Long
Way: Explaining Why Gratitude Expressions Motivate Pro-
social Behavior." *Journal of Personality and Social Psychology,*
Vol. 98, No.6 (2010): 946–955. https://doi.org/10.1037/a0017935.

CHAPTER 9

LinkedIn, "About section." Last modified October 17, 2021. https://
about.linkedin.com/.

CHAPTER 10

Carboni, Inga, Rob Cross, Aaron Page, and Andrew Parker. "Network Drivers of Success: How Successful Women Manage Their
Networks." *Connected Commons,* September 2019.

Mobley, Katherine. "Understanding The Impact of Mentorship
Versus Sponsorship." Forbes, September 17, 2019. https://www.
forbes.com/sites/forbescommunicationscouncil/2019/09/17/
understanding-the-impact-of-mentorship-versus-sponsor-
ship/?sh=6c00435040ad.

CHAPTER 11

Moss Kanter, Rosebeth. *Confidence: How Winning Streaks and Losing Streaks Begin and End.* New York: Three Rivers Press, 2006.

Moss Kanter, Rosebeth. "Over the Eight Barriers to Confidence." *Harvard Business Review,* January 3, 2014. https://hbr.org/2014/01/overcome-the-eight-barriers-to-confidence.

Tabaka, Marla. "New Study Says This Simple Step Will Increase the Odds of Achieving Your Goals (Substantially)." *Inc,* January 28, 2019. https://www.inc.com/marla-tabaka/this-study-found-1-simple-step-to-practically-guarantee-youll-achieve-your-goals-for-real.html.

Made in the USA
Las Vegas, NV
23 August 2023

76463816R00069